Canning & Preserving

Canning & Preserving

Linda Ferrari

Friedman Group

A FRIEDMAN GROUP BOOK

Copyright © 1992 by Michael Friedman Publishing Group, Inc.

ISBN 0-7924-5773-0

CANNING AND PRESERVING
was prepared and produced by
Michael Friedman Publishing Group, Inc.
15 West 26th Street
New York, New York 10010

Editor: Dana Rosen
Art Direction: Devorah Levinrad
Designer: Stephanie Bart-Horvath
Photography Editor: Anne K. Price

Typeset by Miller & Debel, Inc.
Color separation by United South Seas Graphic Art Co. Ltd.
Printed and bound in Hong Kong by Leefung-Asco Printers Ltd.

Every effort has been made to present the information in this book in a clear, complete, and accurate manner. It is important that all instructions be carefully followed, as failure to do so could result in injury. The publisher and the author expressly disclaim any and all liability from improper preparation.

TABLE OF CONTENTS

DEDICATION

This book is for my mom, Evelyn Walker,
my husband, Phil, and my children,
Philip, Michelle, Cindy, Suzy, Carrie,
and T.J., all of whom make my life joyful
and make me feel blessed.

ACKNOWLEDGMENTS

I would like to give a special thanks to all my wonderful friends who have bravely tried out many of my new experimental recipes. Especially Patti Coupe, Sue Perry-Smith, Jill Presson, Gail Carroll, Cindy Daniels and Linda Hanley.

A heartfelt thanks goes to Dr. George York, from the University of California, Davis, for his willingness to give me valuable information concerning my work at any time.

I also want to thank Sharon Kalman, who was my editor at the beginning of this project, but who has since married and moved on to other things. And a personal thanks to my new editor, Dana Rosen, who has since taken over the project and has skillfully kept things running smoothly.

INTRODUCTION

In the last few years there has been a surge of interest in home preserving. A process used for survival a century ago, preserving is now a creative and money-saving hobby.

The preserving process began to be seriously scrutinized at the end of the eighteenth century. Napoléon was looking for a safe way to preserve food for his army troops because many men had died from illnesses related to malnutrition and spoiled food. He challenged a French chef and scientist, Nicolas Appert, to find ways of processing food that would be healthy. Appert experimented for several years and discovered ways of applying heat and sealing containers that had never been thought of before. Because of his experiments and the insights of others — like Louis Pasteur, who realized air needed to be eliminated so microorganisms would not appear, and Samuel Prescott and William Underwood, who applied theories of bacteriology to the preserving process — we are now able to put up foods so they stay edible for long periods of time.

I remember my grandmother preserving everything she could get her hands on. She would work for hours, as she prepared dozens of jars of food. There were baskets full of raspberries, blackberries, apricots, and peaches all over the kitchen and pantry. Grandma would work until all the fruit was put up. I still have visions of how beautiful her pantry looked when it was full of all the different-sized jars filled with glorious colors of fruits and jams.

When I first married, I thought how I would love to have that great supply of food to share with friends and use year-round, like Grandma had — but it was so much work and so messy. Now I preserve many foods every year and I must say that I am able to turn out quite a few quarts in only an hour or so. With all the new appliances that are available, like food processors, blenders, slicers, and dishwashers, life is so much easier than it was for my grandmother. So now I, too, fill my larder with jar after jar of different fruits, vegetables, jams, and jellies. I also enjoy making and using all different kinds of vinegars and oils.

With all these wonderful foods and condiments, I can have fun cooking creatively, using all these different treasures. I have included several recipes for appetizers, main courses, and desserts using each preserved item, and I'm sure you'll find many other imaginative ways to use them as well.

CHAPTER 1
THE BASICS

I am very lucky because I have several fruit trees that bear fruit profusely. It is surprising how much produce you can get from a few well-cared-for trees and a small vegetable garden. If you don't have a corner in your yard for a vegetable garden, you should try growing vegetables in containers. There are now many bush varieties of cucumbers, zucchini, and beans that do very well in containers. If you give them a little care, you'll be amazed at how much four or five potting containers can yield.

If you don't have a garden (and I don't want you to think you have to go through all that work), there are several ways to buy fresh fruits and vegetables. Depending on the amount you want to preserve, you can just buy a few pounds from your grocery store, or you can go to a local farmer's market in your area, where you can get some great buys. You will find it is much cheaper to buy in quantity: by the lug, bushel, or crate. Check your local newspaper to find out what farms are selling what produce. Many of these

© James Church/FPG International

farms will let you pick your own produce, and depending on how ambitious you are, this can save you a lot of money.

Wherever you get your produce, make sure it is firm, crisp, and ripe. Your preserved foods are only as good as the produce with which you start. Once you get your produce, it is important to put it up as soon as possible for optimum freshness.

FOOD SPOILAGE

When putting up fruits and vegetables, it is very important to follow timing and preserving procedures carefully. Botulism is a very serious illness caused by spoiled food. It can be fatal and is very hard to detect.

To prevent botulism, there are safety precautions you can take to ensure that your food is safe.

1. Start by always following directions carefully for each food you put up. Processing times and acid levels change depending on the food being preserved.

2. Don't skip any steps in preparing your food, or jars, and be sure to seal the jars correctly.

3. After the food has been prepared, sealed, processed, and cooled, check to be sure your lids have sealed. The flat lid will be slightly concave. While the jars were cooling, you may have heard popping noises—the heat in the jar produces a vacuum, and this seals the jar, producing a popping sound. Check the lid by slightly pressing down on it. It should not move or make a sound.

4. If you have a few jars that have not sealed properly, refrigerate them and use them as soon as possible.

5. When you use your preserved foods, always listen for a pop when you open the jar.

6. If the food is mushy, moldy, or smells funny, immediately discard the jar and its contents and thoroughly wash your hands. If you are not sure it is spoiled, but it looks funny, throw it out and *do not taste it*.

Bacteria exists in all fresh food. We use the preserving process to inhibit the growth of the bacteria in the food we put up. A high acid content also helps to inhibit bacterial growth, so foods high in acid (fruits or tomatoes) or foods to which acid has been added (pickles, etc.) can be processed in a hot water bath. Foods with a low acid content (vegetables and meats) must be processed at very high heat to retard the bacterial growth. These foods use the pressure cooker to achieve such high levels of heat.

EQUIPMENT

You may think preserving is more difficult than it really is. Actually, it is fun and easy. You don't have to be a great cook to be able to put foods up; you just have to follow a few steps carefully. Once you have gone through the process a few times, you will be able to do it quickly and enjoy the results.

Beginners may want to start off with fruits and jams, since most of the equipment you will need for these recipes is probably already in your kitchen. There are some special tools that make preserving easier, but I would try the process first with the equipment you have and see how inspired you get. I am sure that after you have a few rave reviews of your preserved foods, you will want to try more.

Jars: First of all, I do not recommend that you use commercial jars that have previously contained mayonnaise, peanut butter, or other store-bought foods. The reason I say this is that the seal was broken when you opened the jar, and you need a new seal every time a jar is used for preserving. The preserving lids you buy from the stores usually won't fit these jars. Also, many of these jars are not tempered and will not withstand the temperature needed for preserving. However, my Aunt Thelma does use recycled commercial jars for jams and jellies and seals them with paraffin. This works great for her, but you must be very careful that the jar doesn't break.

Instead, I recommend that you use Ball or Kerr jars; you can get the lids and jars at almost any grocery or hardware store. These jars are made specifically for preserving and can withstand the temperature changes that occur during the preserving process.

Jars come in many sizes and shapes, but all have either "regular" or "wide-mouth" openings. The regular-sized opening is usually the choice for jams and jellies, and the wide-mouth size is used for fruits and vegetables because of the larger pieces of food.

The jars are sealed with a screw-on ring that holds a flat lid with a rubber seal. The screw-on rings can be used over and over again as long as you check them carefully before each use and discard any that have become rusty or bent. Flat sealing lids need to be new each time you use them to ensure a proper seal. If you are using the clamp-type jar, make sure you always have new rubber rings for each jar.

Your mother or grandmother may have old preserving jars you can use. I have some that are years old. They can be used over and over again—just make sure

11

you check for nicks or cracks, discarding any damaged jars. Wash all your jars and screw-on bands in the dishwasher or by hand. Then fill a roasting pan half-full of water and have it simmering on the stove with the uncovered jars upside down in the water. A little saucepan half-full of boiling water can be used to boil the flat metal lids or rubber rings for one to two minutes right before sealing. This helps you get a tight seal.

Canners: Different foods call for different kinds of canners. High-acid fruits and tomatoes use a *Water Bath Canner*. This is a large enameled metal pan that has a rack in it that holds seven jars. It is about three or four inches higher than the jars, so at least one to two inches of water can cover the jars while processing. Any large pot that will accommodate the jars in this fashion can be used. Make sure a rack will fit in the bottom for proper air circulation and that the pan has a lid to help control evaporation.

Pressure Canners produce a heat high enough to use for low-acid foods such as vegetables, meat, fish, and poultry. These are made of heavy-gauge metal and have a flat rack on the floor of the pan. The canner has a clamp lid that makes it steam tight. The lid has a weight gauge (usually five to ten and fifteen pounds), a vent (or petlock), and a pressure safety valve. Make sure you follow the manufacturer's directions carefully when using and cleaning the pressure canner. These canners are costly but will last for years.

The *Steam Canner* can be used like a water bath canner and is used only for fruits and tomatoes. It has a large lid that comes down over the jars and fits into a shallow base that holds six to eight cups of water. It is fitted with a rack that can hold up to seven quart jars. You must make sure the water is boiling before putting the jars in. Steam will flow from the two holes on the side of the lid. Once the water boils and the jars are in, turn the heat down, making sure a stream of steam is still flowing from the holes in the lid. Use the same timing schedule that you use for the water bath canner.

Utensils: You probably already have many of the following items in your kitchen: measuring cups and spoons; sharp paring knives; ladles; slotted spoons; vegetable brushes; large bowls; a colander; a large metal spoon for skimming foam off jams and jellies; a minute timer; scales; a wide-mouth funnel; tongs; a clip thermometer; a blender; a food processor or a grinder; and lots of dish towels. You may not have all of these things, and certain items, like the blender and food processor, are not absolutely necessary. If you do have a blender or processor, use it for slicing, chopping, grinding, or puréeing; it will make things so much simpler.

A few other things you will need and probably won't have are a jar lifter (to help remove hot jars from boiling water); a jelly bag (which drains the juice from fruit for jams and jellies); a cherry pitter; an apple corer; and some labels for noting the contents of the jar and the date you put it up.

PACKING YOUR JARS

There are two packing methods used in preserving, *Raw* or *Cold Packing* and *Hot Packing*. To raw pack, put the food raw into a jar and pour boiling liquid or syrup over the food. To hot pack, cook the food in the boiling liquid or syrup and then use this same liquid for packing the jars.

When hot packing, the food will shrink before filling the jars, so pack tightly. When raw packing, the food will shrink and rise during the processing time; therefore you want to pack the jars very tightly so you won't have only liquid on the bottom. Leave a headspace of one-quarter to one-half inch between the liquid and the lid.

Pack the food in a very hot jar and release all the air bubbles by inserting a butter knife at the side of the jar. Clean the rim of the jar and place a hot lid on it, then firmly screw the metal ring on each jar. Process according to the directions given in the recipe. Never fix more jars than will fit into your preserving device at one time and process immediately after filling. If the jars lose their heat, they will crack and break when put into the processing water.

After processing, remove the jars and place on a clean towel or a wood surface to cool. If a pressure device is used, remove it from the heat until the pressure gauge falls to zero. Open the pressure device, being careful of the steam as you remove the lid. Leave the jars to cool in the device for twenty minutes and then remove. Follow the directions that come with your pressure device carefully. When the jars are cool, test the seal, label, and store in a cool, dark place.

13

CHAPTER 2
*F*RUITS

Fruits are so plentiful all summer long that you have lots of time to catch the

essence of summer in a lovely jar of preserves, whole fruits, or vegetables. You will have

a great feeling of accomplishment when you look at all the jars of preserved foods.

This book begins with some recipes for fruits, jams, jellies, preserves, and

conserves. I have followed each basic recipe with recipes that will include, as an

ingredient, the food you have preserved. I hope this will give you ideas on how to use

your preserved fruits to their fullest advantage. I am sure you will devise many recipes of

your own, which will give you more incentive to preserve your favorite foods.

I start this section with whole fruits that are put up in a syrup.

The syrup can be light, medium, or heavy depending on the amount of sugar you add.

The basic measurements are:

Light:	4 cups water, 2 cups sugar
Medium:	4 cups water, 3 cups sugar
Heavy:	4 cups water, 4¾ cups sugar

Fruits preserved in syrup are delicious eaten as they are, but you can also incorporate them into other dishes. It will take you no time to make a tart or pie, or top your favorite cheesecake when the fruit is already cut and spiced.

Butters are puréed fruit with added sugar and spices that you cook slowly and for a long time until the fruit thickens. I have given the recipe for peach butter, but you can substitute any fruit you want. Apples, plums, and apricots are some of the other fruits that make nice butters.

Jams and *preserves* are next. They are prepared in a similar manner. To make jams, you crush or chop the fruit and cook it to a smooth consistency. To make preserves, the fruit is left in larger chunks and cooled to a soft, spreadable consistency. I love preserves because the fruit suspended in the jar is so beautiful to look at. *Jellies* are done differently because they are made with only the juice of the fruit and are not as thick as jam or preserves.

I also include some *conserves*, which are made by mixing two or more fruits and adding nuts or raisins; and *marmalades*, which are clear jellies with suspended slivers of citrus fruit. You can use any citrus or combination of citrus slivers to make your marmalade. All these fruit preserves are cooked to the jell point, which is 220°F, or boiled using pectin as the jelling agent. In this case, follow the directions on the package of the pectin or in the recipe.

Freezer jam is a fresh-tasting jam that requires no cooking. It is made by cooking the pectin and then stirring it into the fruit mixture. The jam is then stored in the freezer until you use it. Once it is opened, it can be stored in the refrigerator.

In these recipes for fruit preserves, jams, jellies, marmalades, conserves, and fruit butters, I do not always recommend processing in a hot water bath. If you want absolute assurance of a good seal, then process in a hot water bath for ten minutes. However, it really isn't necessary because the preserves are brought to the boiling point and the jars you are filling are hot; when you seal the jars and the preserves begin to cool, the lids pull in and seal. You will hear popping sounds as the jars cool, assuring you that the jar is sealing. Remember this procedure is for preserves only—process the fruits that you intend to put up in syrup for the recommended length of time.

Fruit	How to Prepare	Processing Time	
		Pint	Quart
		minutes	
Apples	Pare, cut in halves or quarters, and trim off core. To keep from darkening, dip in 1 gallon of water that contains 2 tablespoons each of salt and vinegar. Drain. Cook in hot syrup for 2 to 4 minutes, according to the variety. Pack hot. Cover with hot liquid. Seal.	15	15
Applesauce	Wash, pare, if desired, quarter, and core cooking apples. Simmer, covered, in a small amount of water until tender. Press through sieve or food mill. Sweeten if desired. Reheat to boiling and pack into hot jars. Add 1 tablespoon lemon juice to the top of each jar. Seal.	20	20
Apricots	Choose firm, well-colored apricots that are not overripe. To peel, dip in boiling water for 1 minute, then plunge into cold water and peel, or preserve apricots without peeling. Leave whole, or cut in halves and remove pits. *To pack hot:* Bring to a boil in liquid and just heat through or cook about 1 to 3 minutes. Pack hot and cover with hot liquid. Seal. *To pack raw:* Fill the jars with uncooked apricots. Cover with boiling liquid. Seal.	20 25	20 30
Berries other than strawberries	Drain well after washing. For firm berries, add ½ cup sugar to each quart of fruit. Cover pan, bring to a boil, and shake pan to keep fruit from sticking. Pack hot and cover with hot liquid. Seal. For red raspberries and other soft berries, fill jars with raw fruit and shake down for a full pack. Cover with boiling syrup made with juice or water (½ cup sugar and about ¾ cup juice for each quart). Seal.	10 10	10 15
Cherries	Wash, remove stems, sort for size and ripeness, and pit if desired. If left whole, prick to help prevent splitting. *To pack hot:* For pitted cherries, follow directions for firm berries. For cherries with pits, follow directions for firm berries but add a little water to prevent sticking or bring to a boil in hot syrup. Pack hot. Seal. *To pack raw:* Pack into hot jars. Cover with boiling syrup or juice. Seal.	15 20	15 25
Figs	Use tree-ripened figs that are not overripe. Sort and wash. Bring to a boil in hot water. Let stand in the hot water for 3 to 4 minutes. Drain. Pack hot into hot jars. Add 1 tablespoon of lemon juice to each 1-quart jar. Cover with boiling liquid. Do not use baking soda in preparing figs. Seal.	90	90
Grapefruit	Use thoroughly ripened fruit. Peel. Separate segments and peel them. Pack segments in jars. Cover with hot syrup. Seal.	20	25
Grapes	Use ripe muscat or slightly underripe seedless grapes for preserving. Remove stems and wash. *To pack hot:* Bring to a boil in a small amount of liquid. Pack hot into hot jars. Cover with the hot liquid. Seal. *To pack raw:* Put into hot jars and cover with boiling liquid. Seal.	15 20	15 20
Nectarines	Follow directions for freestone peaches.		
Oranges	For Valencia or mandarin oranges, follow directions for grapefruit. Other orange varieties are not recommended because they become bitter.		

17

Fruit	How to Prepare	Processing Time	
		Pint	Quart
		minutes	
Peaches	To peel all except preserving varieties of clingstones, dip in boiling water for about 1 minute, plunge into cold water, then slip off skins. Cut into halves and remove pits. To keep from darkening, dip in 1 gallon of water that contains 2 tablespoons each of salt and vinegar. Drain at once. Peel preserving varieties of clingstone peaches as you would apples, preferably with a stainless steel knife. Once peeled, a cut around the peach and a twisting motion between the hands will remove one-half the fruit from the pit. You can remove the pit from the second half with a special spoon-shaped knife or cut it out carefully with a paring knife.		
	To pack hot: If fruit is juicy, add ½ cup sugar to each quart of raw fruit. Bring to a boil. Drop less juicy fruit into a medium-thin syrup that is boiling hot. Just heat through. Pack hot. Cover with boiling liquid. Seal.		
	Clingstone	20	25
	Freestone	15	20
	To pack raw: Pack in jars with the cut side down and the edges overlapping. Cover with boiling liquid. Seal.		
	Clingstone	25	30
	Freestone	20	25
Pears	Ripen pears for preserving after picking. Do not allow them to become too soft. Pare, cut in halves, and trim out cores.		
	To pack hot: Same as for less juicy peaches. Seal.	15	20
	To pack raw: Same as for peaches. Seal.	20	25
Pineapple	Pare firm but ripe pineapple. Slice crosswise or cut into wedges. Remove the core and trim "eye." Simmer pineapple in light syrup or pineapple juice until tender.		
	To pack hot: Pack hot slices or wedges (spears) into hot jars. Cover with hot cooking liquid leaving ½-inch headspace. Seal.	15	20
Plums and fresh prunes	Sort, remove stems, and wash. If preserving whole, prick to help prevent bursting, or cut into halves.		
	To pack hot: Bring to a boil in juice or in a thin to medium syrup. Pack hot. Cover with boiling liquid. Seal.	15	15
	To pack raw: Pack the fruit into the jar. Cover with boiling juice or syrup. Seal.	20	20
Rhubarb	Cut into ½-inch lengths. Add ½ cup sugar to each quart of rhubarb and let stand 3 to 4 hours to draw out juice. Bring to a boil. Pack hot. Cover with hot juice. Seal.	10	10
Strawberries	Not recommended because the product is usually not satisfactory.		
Tomatoes	Sort, picking out any that are spoiled or green. Do not can overripe tomatoes. They may be too low in acid for safe water bath preserving. Dip in boiling water long enough to crack skins (about 1 minute). Dip in cold water. Peel and remove cores. Save any juice to add to the tomatoes when heating.		
	To pack hot: Bring whole, peeled tomatoes to a boil. Pack immediately into hot jars. Cover with the hot liquid in which the tomatoes were heated. Add 1 teaspoon salt and 2 teaspoons vinegar or 2 teaspoons bottled lemon juice to each quart. Seal.	15	15
	To pack raw: Pack raw, whole, peeled tomatoes tightly to the tops of hot jars. Press tomatoes down after each two tomatoes are added to release juice and to fill spaces. Add 1 teaspoon salt and 2 teaspoons vinegar or 2 teaspoons bottled lemon juice to each quart. Seal.	30	30

© Alison Miksch

Spiced Apples

These apples are delicious eaten right from the jar, but I suggest you put up several jars and enjoy them in a beautiful baked apple pancake or warm them to serve with pork chops. Just make sure to thicken them first with a little cornstarch. They are also delicious baked in an apple strudel.

10 pounds apples, peeled, cored, and sliced thin
4 cups sugar
4 cups water
2 tablespoons lemon juice

1 teaspoon vanilla
1 tablespoon cinnamon
1 teaspoon nutmeg
½ teaspoon mace

Prepare apples and put them into 2 quarts of water containing 2 table-spoons Fruit Fresh or citrus acid until all fruit is prepared to keep the sliced apples from browning. Make the syrup by adding all the ingredi-ents except the apples to a large pan. Bring the syrup to a boil and stir to dissolve the sugar. Rinse the citrus acid solution off the apples, drain, and add the apples to the syrup. Cook the apples 3 to 4 minutes or until they are slightly tender. Remove the pan from heat and spoon the apples and syrup into hot jars. Pack tightly or the apples will float to the top of the jar after processing. Release air bubbles and clean rims. Seal and process in a hot water bath for 15 minutes. Makes 5 quarts.

Apple Strudel

I like to make apple strudel for breakfast on Christmas morning, and having the apples ready makes this special breakfast quick and easy to prepare. You can make this and freeze it uncooked, then bake whenever you wish.

1 quart Spiced Apples
1 package phyllo dough
6 tablespoons unsalted butter, melted
⅓ cup walnuts, chopped finely
Confectioner's sugar

Preheat oven to 375°F.

Drain Spiced Apples. Unfold phyllo and cover it with a damp cloth. Lay one sheet on a flat surface so that it has a rectangular shape. Brush the phyllo with melted butter. Repeat with 7 more sheets, brushing each sheet with butter and stacking the sheets on top of each other. Place the drained apples length-wise near the bottom of the phyllo, and sprinkle the apples with the nuts. Tuck in the ends of the phyllo and roll the pastry jelly-roll fashion. Carefully put the roll on a parchment-lined cookie sheet, seam side down, and brush the top of the phyllo with butter. Bake 15 minutes then brush with more butter. Return to oven and cook for an addi-tional 10 to 15 minutes or until nicely browned. When you remove it from the oven, brush one more time with butter. When slightly cool, dust with confec-tioner's sugar and serve warm. Serves 6 to 8.

19

Cherry Crisp

You can serve this with a cloud of fresh whipped cream.

1 quart **Cherries in Almond Syrup**
2 tablespoons cornstarch
2 tablespoons lemon juice
⅓ cup flour
Pinch of salt
1 teaspoon baking powder
1 egg, beaten
¾ cup brown sugar
¼ cup oats
⅓ cup ground almonds
1 teaspoon cinnamon
¼ teaspoon nutmeg
⅓ cup butter

Preheat oven to 350°F.

Put cherries in a saucepan. In a separate bowl, mix cornstarch and lemon juice, then add to cherries. Heat until cherries thicken, then pour into a greased 9-inch baking dish.

Combine flour, salt, and baking powder. Mix beaten egg into flour with a fork. Sprinkle this mixture over cherries.

Combine brown sugar, oats, almonds, cinnamon, and nutmeg. Cut in butter. Sprinkle this mixture over flour mixture. Bake in a 350°F oven for 40 to 45 minutes, or until golden brown. Serves 8.

Cherry Bundles

These little bundles are beautiful tied together with strips of softened orange peel and set in a pool of vanilla cream.

2½ tablespoons cornstarch
1 quart **Cherries in Almond Syrup**
8 strips orange peel

This Cherry Crisp, with its crunchy topping, tastes especially delicious warm from the oven.

20

Cherries in Almond Syrup

I can't put up enough cherries for my husband; he would eat a quart every night. If you plan on doing many jars of these, it would be worth investing in a cherry pitter.

12 **pounds bing cherries**   1 teaspoon almond extract
4¾ cups sugar   ¼ cup lemon juice
4 cups water

Wash and pit all the cherries. In a large pan, bring to a boil the sugar, water, almond extract, and lemon juice. Put cherries into hot jars and fill with syrup to within ½ inch of the rim of the jar. Release air bubbles, clean rims, and seal. Process in a hot water bath for 20 minutes for pints and 30 minutes for quarts. Makes 4 to 5 quarts.

24 sheets phyllo dough
1½ cups unsalted butter, melted
1 cup whipping cream
3 tablespoons sugar
2 teaspoons vanilla
Confectioner's sugar

Preheat oven to 400°F. Mix cornstarch with some of the Almond Syrup and blend well. Put cherries into a saucepan and add cornstarch mixture. Cook until thickened. Set aside.

Take a lemon zester or knife and cut pieces of orange peel from around the width of an orange. Boil the peel for 10 minutes. Set aside.

Lightly brush 3 sheets of phyllo with butter. (Be sure to keep unused phyllo covered with a damp cloth or it will dry out.) Fold phyllo in half widthwise.

Place a scant ½ cup of cherries in the center of the phyllo. Pull 4 corners of the phyllo up and gather above the cherries, leaving 2 inches of phyllo at top of cherries. Carefully tie the orange peel where you squeezed the phyllo and fluff phyllo above the tie to look like a flower. Brush the entire bundle with butter and place on a rimmed cookie sheet lined with parchment paper. Repeat until all are made. Place in 400°F oven 30 to 40 minutes, or until golden brown.

Whip the cream, sugar, and vanilla until it just begins to thicken; you want it the consistency of a thick milk shake.

Serve the warm Cherry Bundle in a pool of the vanilla cream with a little confectioner's sugar sprinkled on the bundle. Serves 8.

21

Cherry Kirsch Sauce served over ice cream makes a quick and delicious dessert.

Cherry Kirsch Sauce for Ice Cream

I really like the taste of chocolate and cherries together, so I serve this sauce on ice cream that is sitting on top of a brownie. It is scrumptious if the brownie and sauce are warm and the ice cream is very cold.

1 pint Cherries in Almond Syrup
2 teaspoons cornstarch
1 tablespoon cherry kirsch
¼ cup chopped almonds, toasted

Put cherries in a saucepan. In a mixing bowl, combine cornstarch with 2 tablespoons of the Almond Syrup. When smooth, mix into cherries and heat, stirring until it thickens slightly. Stir in kirsch and almonds.

Makes 2¼ cups, or 9 servings. Will keep, refrigerated, for up to 2 weeks.

Seedless Raspberry Jam

You may think it foolish to remove the seeds from your raspberries. If so, then just leave the seeds in and follow the same proportions for the jam. To remove the seeds, you can use a food processor attachment, or you can push the raspberries through a fine mesh sieve for equally good results.

6 cups raspberry pulp
(approximately 12 boxes
fresh raspberries)

2 ounces pectin
8½ cups sugar
¼ teaspoon butter (optional)

Crush berries and remove seeds (if desired). Measure pulp to be sure you have 6 cups. Put pulp into a large saucepan, add the pectin, and stir to dissolve. Bring the mixture to a boil. Add the sugar and stir to dissolve. Add the butter if you wish (it helps keep the foam down). Bring the mixture to a rolling boil that cannot be stirred down. Boil for exactly 4 minutes. Remove from heat and skim off any foam. Ladle into jars, clean rims, and seal. Makes 8 half-pint jars.

22

Cake:
1½ cups sugar
⅓ cup Chambord
1½ cups semisweet chocolate chips
1½ teaspoons instant espresso powder
1½ teaspoons vanilla
9 tablespoons unsalted butter,
   softened
12 egg yolks
1½ cups ground walnuts
3 tablespoons bread crumbs
12 egg whites
¼ teaspoon salt

Preheat oven to 350°F.

Butter a jelly-roll pan and line with parchment paper. Butter the paper and dust with flour.

Put sugar, Chambord, chocolate chips, espresso powder, and vanilla in a saucepan and stir until melted. Set aside and cool. Cream butter and add egg yolks one at a time until all are

White Chocolate and Raspberry Brownies

If your family loves brownies, they will enjoy this rich white chocolate brownie.

8 ounces white chocolate
1 cup unsalted butter, softened
½ cup Seedless Raspberry Jam
1 teaspoon vanilla
1½ cups flour
1 cup sugar
4 eggs, beaten
¾ cup white chocolate chips
1 cup macadamia nuts

Preheat oven to 350°F.

Butter a 9 x 13-inch pan.

Melt chocolate in your microwave oven or in the top of a double boiler over simmering water. Add butter, jam, and vanilla to melted chocolate. Stir until butter melts. Combine flour and sugar in a bowl and add chocolate mixture and beaten eggs. Blend until dry ingredients are just moistened. Stir in white chocolate chips and nuts. Spread in greased pan and bake for 35 to 38 minutes. Cool and cut into squares.

Chocolate Raspberry Torte

This is without a doubt a spectacular cake. It is rich-tasting and well worth every second it takes to make. This cake developed when I was having a party for a special friend, Sue Perry-Smith, and I wanted a special dessert.

© Henryk T. Kaiser/Envision

23

blended. Beat in cooled chocolate mixture, ground walnuts, and bread crumbs. Beat 3 minutes. Beat egg whites with salt until stiff. Fold in chocolate mixture. Spread in prepared pan and bake for 20 to 25 minutes. Cool 15 minutes and turn out on rack and remove paper. Cool completely.

Filling:
1⅓ cups semisweet
   chocolate chips
⅓ cup Seedless Raspberry Jam
4 teaspoons instant espresso powder
1¼ cups unsalted butter, softened
3 egg yolks
1 cup confectioner's sugar
½ cup whipping cream

Melt the chocolate chips, Raspberry Jam, and espresso powder in a double boiler or microwave. Cool. Cream butter

and beat in egg yolks one at a time. Beat in confectioner's sugar and cooled chocolate mixture. Whip cream and fold into chocolate mixture.

Glaze:
12 ounces chocolate chips
¾ cup unsalted butter
2 tablespoons light corn syrup
1 teaspoon instant espresso powder

Garnish:
Seedless Raspberry Jam
Fresh raspberries

Put the chocolate chips, butter, corn syrup, and espresso powder in a large measuring cup and microwave or melt in a double boiler. Mix until very smooth. Keep mixing until the glaze begins to thicken, 3 to 5 minutes.

To assemble, cut cake into 3 equal pieces. Put one piece on a platter.

Spread a thin layer of the Raspberry Jam on the cake. Top with a layer of the filling (about 1½ cups). Put on another layer of the cake and repeat with the jam and filling. Top with last layer of cake. To keep your plate clean when applying glaze, put strips of wax paper along sides and ends of cake, tucking paper under cake a little if you can. Pour the glaze carefully onto the cake with a large spoon. Use a knife and try to get it on the sides of the cake. (It will drip down so spread it as it does.) When the cake is all covered, refrigerate 10 minutes and then remove the wax paper. Refrigerate at least 2 hours before serving. Before serving, encircle the cake with the fresh raspberries and refrigerate until served. Serves 12 to 14.

Chicken and Pasta with Raspberry Sauce

Please don't let the thought of raspberries on your pasta scare you from trying this recipe. This is a wonderful blend of flavors and makes a very impressive first course.

2 chicken breasts
½ cup white wine
4 tablespoons unsalted butter
3 tablespoons minced onion
2 tablespoons minced celery
1 tablespoon fresh minced parsley
3 tablespoons pine nuts
1½ teaspoons pepper
1 teaspoon salt
¼ cup sour cream
¾ cup cream
3 tablespoons Seedless Raspberry Jam
1 teaspoon thyme
1 tablespoon lemon juice
9 ounces pasta
Parmesan cheese (to taste)

Simmer chicken breasts in ½ cup white wine and water to cover until tender. Remove skin and dice into large pieces. Melt butter in a pan and sauté onion, celery, parsley, and pine nuts until onions are transparent. Add pepper, salt, sour cream, cream, Raspberry Jam, thyme, and lemon juice. Blend well and cook until heated through. Do not boil. Add chicken and cook 1 minute more.

Cook pasta in salted, boiling water. Drain and add hot chicken sauce. Sprinkle with Parmesan cheese. Makes 4 main course servings or 6 first courses.

© Burke/Triolo

A platter of these delicious ribs, cooked with Plum Barbecue Sauce, will satisfy anyone's hunger.

Plum Jam with Chambord

This is a delicious jam with a beautiful color.

4½ pounds plums or 6 cups plum pulp	¼ cup lemon juice
½ cup Chambord	2 ounces pectin
	8½ cups sugar

Halve, pit, and chop the plums, coarsely, or grind in food processor. Measure 6 cups pulp. Put the pulp in a large, deep pan. Add Chambord, lemon juice, and pectin. Stir the mixture until the pectin is dissolved, then bring to a boil. Add sugar and stir to dissolve. Bring mixture to a rolling boil that cannot be stirred down. Boil exactly 4 minutes. Remove from heat and skim off any foam that may have formed. Ladle into hot jars, clean rims, and seal with hot lids. Process in a hot water bath for 10 minutes. Makes 8 half-pint jars.

Plum Barbecue Sauce

Whenever I make ribs, I precook them to get rid of the fat. Boil pork ribs for about 20 minutes, drain them, and then put them on the barbecue for 15 minutes or cut them up in a roasting pan and place them in the oven at 350°F for 1½ hours. Bake beef ribs in the oven for about 30 minutes at 400°F. Drain off any fat before adding sauce and then barbecue for 15 minutes or bake at 375°F for 35 to 45 minutes. Cooking the ribs in the oven with lots of the sauce poured over them makes for very tender, succulent meat. I prefer it to the barbecue.

48 ounces ketchup
8 ounces Plum Jam with Chambord
½ cup brown sugar
½ cup Chambord
¾ cup strawberry vinegar
4 bay leaves, crushed
1 teaspoon cracked pepper

Mix all ingredients well in a large pan and cook, stirring, until sugar is dissolved. Proceed as described above, removing fat from ribs, then cooking on the barbecue or in the oven. Sauce can be frozen. Makes about 8 cups, enough sauce for 10 to 12 pounds of ribs.

Blueberry-Lemon Jam

This jam is fantastic on hot scones, but I also love it in a sauce that can be used on duck or squab.

8 cups fresh blueberries	**1 teaspoon lemon extract**
2 tablespoons lemon rind	**3 cups sugar**
2 tablespoons lemon juice	**1 cup honey**

Wash and drain blueberries. Put into a large pot and add the rest of the ingredients. Stir well to dissolve the sugar and bring to a boil. Let the jam boil slowly, stirring occasionally so it doesn't stick, for 20 to 30 minutes until thick, or until a thermometer reads 220°F. Skim any foam from the jam with a metal spoon, and let jam sit for about 5 minutes. Ladle into hot jars, clean rims, and seal with hot lids. Process in a hot water bath for 10 minutes. Makes 4 half-pint jars.

25

Blueberry-Lemon Mousse

This is a marvelous light dessert to end a heavy meal.

8 ounces Blueberry-Lemon Jam
2 tablespoons lemon juice
1½ teaspoons unflavored gelatin
2 tablespoons water
1 teaspoon vanilla
2 tablespoons Chambord
2 egg whites
1 cup heavy cream
1 cup sour cream
2 tablespoons grated lemon zest

Heat the jam and lemon juice in a saucepan until jam liquifies. In a cup put into a pan of boiling water, soften the gelatin with water, stirring until the gelatin dissolves. Mix the gelatin into the melted jam. Mix in vanilla and Chambord. Beat egg whites until stiff, then remove to a large bowl. Put whipping cream and sour cream into the bowl you used to beat egg whites and beat until stiff. Mix the lemon zest and cooled jam into the whipping cream mixture. Carefully fold in the egg whites. Spoon into bowls or crystal glasses. Makes 8 servings.

© Alison Miksch

26

Blueberry Sauce for Duck

This is a good sauce to use on any fowl. I begin by baking the fowl in the oven, and then put the sauce on for the last 20 to 30 minutes of cooking. You can either continue cooking in the oven or finish on the barbecue.

Sauce:
8 ounces Blueberry-Lemon Jam
½ cup lemonade
½ cup brown sugar
1 tablespoon soy sauce
1 teaspoon Worcestershire sauce

Duck:
2 to 3 tablespoons water
Salt to taste
Pepper to taste
4- to 4½-pound duck
Lemon rind
3-inch piece of leek, white part
1 celery stalk

Mix jam, lemonade, brown sugar, soy sauce, and Worcestershire sauce and heat until sugar dissolves.

Preheat oven to 400°F.

Wash and prepare duck, removing any excess fat from the cavity. Salt and pepper the inside of the duck and put a few strips of lemon rind, the leek, and a stalk of celery with the leaves attached inside the cavity. Prick the skin of the duck in several places; this will help some of the fat run off during cooking. Tie the duck and sprinkle the outside with salt and pepper. Bake at 400°F for 10 minutes then turn oven to 350°F and continue to cook for 45 minutes. Remove fat from roasting pan during cooking with a baster to keep your oven from smoking. After the duck has cooked for 55 minutes, brush with the Blueberry-Lemon Sauce and return to the oven for 15 to 30 minutes (depending on how well-done you want your meat). Baste every 5 to 10 minutes with more sauce until the duck is a beautiful mahogany color. Untie trussing, and remove lemon rind, leek, and celery from the cavity. Slice the duck and present it on a platter with a little cup of extra sauce. Serves 4.

Scrumptious Cornish Hens

Serve these cornish hens on a bed of fresh kale. The colors are beautiful.

6 rock cornish hens
Salt to taste
Pepper to taste
¼ cup butter, melted
1 cup Strawberry-Orange Jam
¼ cup Grand Marnier
1 teaspoon crushed rosemary

Preheat oven to 425°F.

Clean the hens inside and out and pat dry. Sprinkle the insides with a little salt and pepper and truss the birds. Brush the hens with butter and sprinkle the outsides with salt and pepper. Roast the hens in a roasting pan for 10 minutes and then reduce the heat to 350°F and continue cooking 40 minutes more. Heat jam, Grand Marnier, and rosemary until the jam liquifies. Baste the hens generously and continue to baste every 10 minutes until the birds are a beautiful brown color, about 20 to 30 minutes more. Serves 6.

Strawberry-Orange Freezer Jam

Freezer jam is very easy to make and requires no cooking. The flavor of fresh fruit really comes out in this jam.

11 ounces drained mandarin oranges, crushed
1½ cups crushed strawberries
4 cups sugar

2 tablespoons lemon juice
1 cup water
2 ounces pectin

Mix together crushed oranges and strawberries. Add sugar and lemon juice and mix well. Let stand for at least 20 minutes. Put water and pectin together in a saucepan and mix thoroughly. Bring mixture to a rolling boil that cannot be stirred down and boil 1 minute. Remove from heat and mix pectin into fruit, stirring constantly for 3 minutes. Ladle into sterilized jars, clean rims, and seal. Let jam set overnight. Store in freezer. Makes 6 half-pint jars.

English Trifle

This dessert always wins rave reviews at any dinner party. It is sumptuous and creamy and very elegant.

1 3-ounce package instant vanilla pudding
1 cup whipping cream
¼ cup confectioner's sugar
1 teaspoon vanilla
8 cups angel food or sponge cake, cut in 1-inch cubes
⅔ cup Grand Marnier
1 cup Strawberry-Orange Jam
Slivered almonds, for garnish

Make pudding according to package directions. Set aside. Whip cream with confectioner's sugar and vanilla until soft peaks form. Mix 1 cup of whipped cream into pudding and blend well. Put half of the cake cubes in the bottom of a 2-quart clear glass bowl. Sprinkle with a few tablespoons of the Grand Marnier.

Spread ½ cup of the jam over the cake, then spread with half of the pudding mixture. Top with the remaining cake cubes. Sprinkle again with Grand Marnier and spread with the remaining jam. Cover with the rest of the pudding and top it all off with the remaining whipped cream, making pretty peaks with the cream. Sprinkle with slivered almonds and refrigerate 6 hours to overnight so the flavors blend. Serves 10.

27

28

Cranberry-Orange Marmalade

When making this marmalade, make sure you use only the outer orange part of the skin; the white part of the orange (the pith) will make the marmalade taste bitter.

3 oranges	2 tablespoons lemon juice
4 cups fresh cranberries	4½ to 5 cups sugar

Wash oranges with a vegetable brush. Remove outer peel from oranges, leaving the pith on the oranges. Set peel aside. Boil in water for 15 minutes and drain. When cool, cut into thin strips.

Squeeze juice from oranges and put into a 3-quart saucepan. Crush cranberries in a food processor and add to orange juice. Add lemon juice and sugar and bring mixture to a boil, stirring constantly. Add orange peel and cook gently until thermometer reads 220°F. Skim off any foam that has formed and let set 5 minutes. Ladle into hot jars, clean rims, and seal with hot lids. Makes 6 half-pint jars.

Cranberry-Orange Waffles

These waffles can be made with any jam, preserve, or marmalade added to the batter, but Cranberry-Orange Marmalade makes them especially delicious, and brightly colorful.

1⅓ cups all-purpose flour
2 teaspoons baking powder
½ teaspoon salt
1 tablespoon sugar
2 teaspoons vanilla
½ cup Cranberry-Orange Marmalade
3 tablespoons vegetable oil
1¼ cups milk
2 eggs, separated

Mix flour, baking powder, salt, and sugar. Add vanilla, marmalade, vegetable oil, milk, and egg yolks. Mix until blended. Beat egg whites until they hold shape and fold into batter. Proceed following the directions of your waffle maker. Serves 6.

Cranberry Crisp

This is really easy and so good. My family likes it served with ice cream.

4 cups fresh cranberries
¾ cup Cranberry-Orange Marmalade
½ cup sugar
1 teaspoon lemon juice
2 teaspoons cornstarch
2 tablespoons Cassis
1 box white cake mix
⅔ cup ground walnuts
1¼ cups butter, melted

Preheat oven to 350°F.

Put cranberries, marmalade, sugar, and lemon juice in a saucepan and mix well. Cook for 8 to 10 minutes or until cranberries soften. Mix cornstarch with Cassis. Pour into cranberry mixture and cook, stirring until it thickens. Put into a 10-inch pie or cake pan.

Mix dry cake mix and ground walnuts together. Sprinkle over cranberries. Pour melted butter as evenly as possible over all and cook for 35 to 45 minutes or until golden brown. Serves 10.

Apricot-Almond Conserve

Use this conserve in your next Christmas Fruitcake, or in Apricot Sticks made with puff pastry. You will love them both.

4½ pounds apricots, pitted and quartered
6 ounces apricot nectar
4 cups sugar
3 tablespoons lemon juice
1 teaspoon ginger
½ teaspoon nutmeg
½ teaspoon cloves
4 ounces slivered almonds

Put prepared apricots in a large saucepan. Add nectar, sugar, lemon juice, ginger, nutmeg, and cloves. Stir until sugar is dissolved and bring to a boil. Boil until a candy thermometer reaches 220°F. Stir in almonds. Remove pan from heat and let sit for five minutes, skimming off any foam that forms. Ladle into hot jars, clean rims, and seal. Makes 5 half-pint jars.

© Guy Powers/Envision

30

When serving this fruitcake, you may want to top it with a simple powdered-sugar glaze.

Apricot Sticks

You can use frozen puff pastry sheets for this recipe and they work great. I always make my own puff pastry using Julia Child's recipe for quick puff pastry, found in her book *Julia Child and Company*. It makes a light, delicious pastry that rises to great heights.

1 box frozen puff pastry (1 pound)
1½ cups Apricot-Almond Conserve
1 egg
1 teaspoon water
Crystallized sugar

Defrost puff pastry in refrigerator overnight.

Preheat oven to 400°F.

Open pastry and cut each square into 4 equal squares. Put 2½ tablespoons of the conserve down the center of each pastry square. Roll the pastry like a cigar. Place on a cookie sheet lined with parchment paper. Continue filling and rolling

pastries until all are done. Beat the egg and water together and brush on the pastries. Refrigerate for 15 minutes. Remove from the refrigerator and brush with egg once more. Sprinkle with crystallized sugar and bake for 18 to 20 minutes or until golden brown. Makes 8.

Christmas Fruitcake

Make this cake early and keep soaking it with brandy as it ages.

1 pound fruitcake mix
½ pound candied cherries
½ pound candied pineapple
½ pound candied citron
½ pound candied orange peel
1 cup chopped pecans
1 cup walnuts, chopped
1 cup blanched almonds
6 ounces dried apricots, diced

8 ounces pitted dates, diced
8 ounces raisins
8 ounces Apricot-Almond Conserve
½ cup dark molasses
1½ cups butter, softened
1 cup brown sugar
5 eggs
1 teaspoon vanilla
¼ cup brandy
¼ teaspoon cloves
½ teaspoon nutmeg
2 teaspoons cinnamon
¼ teaspoon allspice
½ teaspoon salt
3 cups flour
brandy

Preheat oven to 300°F.

Prepare 2 9 x 5 loaf cake pans or 8 3 x 5 loaf pans by buttering them, lining them with wax paper, and then buttering the wax paper. Put fruitcake mix, cherries, pineapple, citron, orange peel, pecans, walnuts, almonds, apricots, dates, and raisins into a large bowl and toss together, mixing well. Put conserve, molasses, butter, sugar, eggs, and vanilla in a separate mixing bowl and beat until smooth. Add brandy, cloves, nutmeg, cinnamon, allspice, salt, and flour and mix well. Fold flour mixture into fruit mixture and blend. Spoon into prepared pans and cook for 2 to 3 hours; when a cake tester comes out clean, the cakes are done. Remove the cakes from the oven and put on a cooling rack, removing the wax paper. Sprinkle the cakes with brandy. When cakes are cool, sprinkle again with brandy and wrap in cheesecloth and then foil. Add brandy again every two weeks until cakes are eaten. Makes 2 9 x 5 loaf cakes or 8 3 x 5 mini loaves.

Peach Butter

Butters are delicious on hot biscuits or toast, but you can also use them in many other ways.

5 pounds peaches
¼ cup lemon juice
12 ounces peach nectar
4 cups sugar
1 cup brown sugar
1 tablespoon cinnamon
1 teaspoon nutmeg
1 teaspoon vanilla

Peel, pit, and purée peaches. Put peaches in a large saucepan and add lemon juice, nectar, sugars, cinnamon, nutmeg, and vanilla. Stir to dissolve sugar. Bring to a slow boil and cook, stirring often, 20 to 30 minutes or until nice and thick. Ladle into hot jars, clean rims, and seal. Process in a hot water bath for ten minutes. Makes 10 half-pint jars.

Peachy French Pancakes

My mom always made these pancakes, and we would just put a little butter in them, roll them up, and put syrup on them. They were wonderful and would melt in your mouth. They are very similar to a crepe and are easy to make.

1 cup flour
1 cup milk
3 tablespoons Crisco
1 egg
1 teaspoon salt
1 cup whipping cream
1 tablespoon sugar
⅓ cup Peach Butter
1 cup finely diced peaches,
   fresh or canned, drained
Powdered sugar

Put flour in a mixing bowl. Warm milk and Crisco until Crisco melts. Add to flour. Then add egg and salt and beat until well blended. Set aside. Whip cream with the sugar until stiff. Stir in Peach Butter and peaches and set aside.

Put a little oil in a frying pan and spread it lightly with a paper towel. When hot, add a couple of tablespoons of batter, turning the pan to spread it very thin. Cook until done and turn over and cook 15 to 20 seconds more. Remove from pan and cook all the pancakes in the same manner. When finished, spread some of the peach cream down the center of each pancake and roll up. Sprinkle lightly with powdered sugar. Makes 12 pancakes.

Peach Nut Bread

Try this fragrant tea bread. It freezes very nicely.

3 eggs
1 cup oil
2 cups brown sugar
2 teaspoons vanilla
1 cup Peach Butter
2 cups flour
1 cup cake flour
1 teaspoon cinnamon
½ teaspoon nutmeg
¼ teaspoon mace
1 teaspoon salt
1 teaspoon baking soda
½ teaspoon baking powder
1 cup walnuts

Preheat oven to 350°F. Grease 4 3 x 5 loaf pans or 1 9 x 5 loaf pan. Mix eggs, oil, sugar, vanilla, and Peach Butter until well blended. Sift flours, cinnamon, nutmeg, mace, salt, soda, and baking powder into egg mixture. Blend well. Fold in walnuts and pour into greased pan(s). Bake 9 x 5 loaf pan for 60 to 70 minutes; bake 3 x 5 loaf pans 35 to 45 minutes. Makes 1 loaf or 4 mini loaves.

31

A moist, fragrant loaf of Peach Nut Bread.

32

Tomatoes

Tomatoes are considered fruits because of their high acid content. Because of this, they are processed in a hot water bath. Tomatoes are at their best in the hot summer months when they are red and juicy. The tomatoes we get from our markets the rest of the year lack flavor and color, and are mushy. So, if you preserve these little treasures in the summer, you can enjoy the wonderful flavor of ripe tomatoes all year round. I preserve 75 to 100 quarts of plain tomatoes that I peel, core, and put whole in jars, adding to each jar 1 teaspoon of salt, 1 teaspoon of sugar, and 1 tablespoon of lemon juice. By pressing down the tomatoes snugly in the jars, you will have enough juice to preserve them in. Then I process them in a hot water bath for 45 minutes.

Steven Mark Needham/Envision

33

Tomato Sauce

This is just a basic tomato sauce to use anytime tomato sauce is called for.

10 pounds tomatoes	2 teaspoons pepper
1 large red pepper, minced	¼ cup lemon juice
1 large onion, minced	½ cup vinegar
1½ tablespoons salt	

Drop a couple of tomatoes at a time in boiling water. Leave for 30 seconds and peel. Core and quarter all tomatoes. Put all ingredients into a large saucepan and cook for 40 minutes. Process in a food processor or blender in batches until all tomatoes and vegetables are liquified. Return to pan and cook 30 minutes more. Ladle into hot jars, clean rims, and seal with hot lids. Process in a hot water bath for 45 minutes. Makes 5 quarts.

Chicken Enchiladas

This is a hearty, flavorful dish. My children love it.

Filling:
¼ cup onion, diced
1 garlic clove, minced
2 tablespoons vegetable oil
3 cups cooked chicken, diced
¼ cup diced chilies
½ teaspoon oregano

Sauté onions and garlic in oil until soft. Add chicken, chilies, and oregano. Mix well and set aside.

Sauce:
½ cup chilies, diced
1 teaspoon fresh cilantro, minced
2 cloves garlic, minced
2 tablespoons oil
1½ tablespoons flour
8 ounces Tomato Sauce
½ teaspoon grandma's pepper
   (chili pepper)
1 teaspoon salt
¼ teaspoon cloves
1 cup chicken broth
1 cup heavy cream

Sauté ¼ cup of the chilies, the cilantro, and garlic in oil. Add flour and cook 1 minute. Add Tomato Sauce, pepper, salt, cloves, the rest of the chilies, and chicken broth. Simmer for 10 minutes. Cool mixture slightly. Purée in a blender or food processor. Return to pan and stir in cream. Heat gently and keep warm.

1 dozen corn tortillas
Oil for frying
Monterey Jack cheese, grated
Sour cream
Green onions
Black olives

34

Preheat oven to 350°F.

Fry each tortilla in oil until soft. Drain on paper towel and quickly dip in sauce. Shake off excess sauce and then fill with a couple spoonfuls of chicken, sprinkle with a little cheese, drizzle a spoonful of sauce over all, and roll. Place seam down in a baking pan. Continue until all tortillas are done.

Spoon some sauce on the tortillas and sprinkle cheese over all. Cover and cook for 15 minutes. Uncover and cook 10 to 15 minutes more or until bubbly. Garnish with sour cream, green onions, and black olives. Makes 12 enchiladas.

Lasagne

Use homemade tomato sauce in this recipe; canned tomato sauce from the supermarket will not have the same light-tasting results.

16 ounces lasagne noodles
2 tablespoons olive oil
1 carrot, minced
1 stalk celery, minced
1 onion, minced

Let this Lasagna sit at least 10 minutes before serving. This dish is a great crowd pleaser.

1½ quarts Tomato Sauce
3 ounces packaged spaghetti
    sauce mix
4 cups cooked chicken, turkey, or
    beef, diced (optional)
2 cups ricotta cheese
10 ounces fresh or frozen spinach
¼ cup Parmesan cheese, grated
Salt to taste
Pepper to taste
3 cups mozzarella and
    cheddar cheeses, mixed
Parmesan cheese, grated

Cook noodles in salted water, drain, and reserve in cold water. Heat oil in large pan and add carrot, celery, and onion. Sauté until vegetables are soft. Add Tomato Sauce and sauce mix and cook for 15 minutes, stirring often. If desired, add meat and cook until meat is hot. Remove from heat. Mix ricotta cheese, spinach, Parmesan cheese, salt, and pepper in a separate bowl.

Preheat oven to 375°F.

Line a 9 x 13 pan with noodles. Spread ½ ricotta mixture over noodles and spoon ⅓ sauce over all. Sprinkle with ⅓ cheese. Add another layer of noodles and repeat with the rest of the ricotta, ⅓ sauce, and ⅓ cheese. Layer with noodles one more time. Top with remaining sauce and cheese. Sprinkle with Parmesan cheese and cover the pan with foil. Bake for 40 minutes. Remove foil and cook an additional 10 to 15 minutes or until lasagne is bubbling and slightly brown. Serves 9 to 12.

© Steven Mark Needham/Envision

You can use any vegetables you have on hand for this Minestrone Soup. Here, we have added zucchini.

Minestrone Soup

The great thing about minestrone soup is that you can add just about any combination of vegetables you have on hand.

1 cup dried white beans
3 tablespoons olive oil
2 onions, minced
2 garlic cloves, minced
¼ cup fresh parsley, minced
4 slices bacon, diced
12 whole tomatoes, diced
1 quart Tomato Sauce
3 quarts water
⅓ cup beef stock
1½ teaspoons marjoram
1½ teaspoons thyme
1 teaspoon pepper
Salt to taste
4 small potatoes, diced
3 carrots, diced
3 stalks celery, diced
1 cup small pasta shells or noodles
1 cup peas
10 ounces fresh or frozen spinach
½ cup cabbage, sliced
Parsley
Parmesan cheese, grated

35

Soak beans overnight. Heat oil in a large stockpot; when hot, add onions, garlic, parsley, and bacon. Cook until vegetables are soft. Add tomatoes, Tomato Sauce, water, beef stock, marjoram, thyme, pepper, and salt. Drain beans and add to mixture. Cover and cook for 2 hours on a low simmer.

Add potatoes and carrots and cook for about 10 minutes. Add celery and noodles. Cook until noodles are soft. Add peas, spinach, and cabbage and cook another 15 minutes. Serve with fresh parsley and Parmesan cheese. Makes about 4 quarts.

Spicy Tomato Sauce

This chunky tomato sauce is very versatile. You can probably think of many ways to use it.

8 pounds tomatoes	2 tablespoons olive oil
1 carrot	¼ cup lemon juice
1 large onion	2 teaspoons celery seed
1 green pepper	1 teaspoon oregano
2 tablespoons fresh parsley	1 teaspoon rosemary
4 garlic cloves	1 teaspoon pepper
8 large fresh basil leaves	3 teaspoons salt
or 1 tablespoon dried	1 teaspoon sugar

Peel and dice tomatoes. Mince the carrot, onion, pepper, parsley, garlic, and basil in a food processor. Heat oil in a large deep saucepan and add all of the ingredients except the tomatoes and spices. Sauté for 4 minutes. Add tomatoes and spices and cook until mixture comes to a slow boil. Cook for 15 minutes, stirring often. Remove from heat and ladle into hot jars. Release air bubbles, clean rims, and seal. Process in a hot water bath for 45 minutes. Makes 7 pints.

36

© Michael A. Keller/FPG International

Spicy Chicken

An all-in-one pan makes clean-up easy. This chicken smells wonderful as it cooks.

1 4-pound whole chicken, cut up
½ cup flour
3 tablespoons olive oil
2 garlic cloves
1 pint Spicy Tomato Sauce
1 pint whole tomatoes, chopped
½ cup white wine
1½ teaspoons oregano
3 tablespoons fresh parsley, minced
1 teaspoon salt
1 teaspoon fresh-ground black pepper
½ pound mushrooms, sliced
½ cup pitted olives
Parmesan cheese, grated

Preheat oven to 350°F.

Wet chicken and dredge in flour, shaking off excess. If you have garlic oil, sauté the chicken in it. If not, use olive oil with a few garlic cloves in the pan. Sauté chicken and remove. Pour oil out of pan, add Spicy Tomato Sauce, whole tomatoes, white wine, oregano, 2 tablespoons parsley, salt, and pepper. Heat through. Add mushrooms and chicken and cook covered in the oven for 30 minutes. Remove cover and add olives. Cook 20 to 25 minutes more. Serve with a sprinkling of parsley and Parmesan cheese. Serves 4.

Swordfish with Tomato Cream Sauce

This is a delicious fish with a beautiful sauce.

4 8-ounce swordfish steaks
2 tablespoons butter, melted
1½ cups Spicy Tomato Sauce
1 tablespoon balsamic vinegar
Juice of one lemon
⅓ cup cream
Salt to taste
Fresh-ground black pepper to taste

Brush swordfish with melted butter on both sides. Broil or grill the fish for 4 minutes on each side. Meanwhile make the sauce. Purée Spicy Tomato Sauce, vinegar, and lemon juice in a blender or food processor, then put this sauce in a saucepan and cook for 3 or 4 minutes over low heat. Blend in cream and season with salt and pepper. Cook about 2 minutes more. Serve sauce over fish. Serves 4.

I use crab legs in my Cioppino because I like the look of the claws. But you can use plain crab or lobster meat if you don't want to bother with the shells.

Cioppino

If you like this recipe, you may want to preserve quart sizes of the Spicy Tomato Sauce.

1 quart Spicy Tomato Sauce
1 6-ounce bottle clam juice
1 cup dry vermouth
2 tablespoons Worcestershire sauce

1 can minced clams
½ pound white fish, cut into 1-inch squares
½ pound peeled shrimp
½ pound scallops
2 large crab legs, cut into thirds
4 to 6 fresh clams

Mix the Spicy Tomato Sauce, clam juice, vermouth, and Worcestershire sauce in a deep narrow pot. Bring mixture to a slow boil and cook, stirring, for 5 minutes. Add clams in their broth and the white fish. Cook 4 minutes. Add the shrimp and cook 4 more minutes. Stir to make sure nothing sticks. Add scallops, crab legs, and clams. Cover pot and cook until clams open, about 5 minutes. Ladle into large soup bowls and serve with homemade French bread. Serves 4.

© Michael Skott

CHAPTER 3
VEGETABLES

Vegetables are wonderful to preserve. Basically, any vegetable can be preserved in salted water. You can make many combinations, but just remember to combine vegetables that need to be processed for the same length of time. Then you can add any spices you like or put them up in plain salted water and spice them when you use them. You can also pickle many vegetables; just make sure the vegetables you start with are fresh and crisp. Your preserved vegetables are only as good as what you start with. Also, it is very important to follow directions very closely for processing times and procedures. Vegetables can spoil easily if not done correctly. A pressure device is used for vegetables except for those that are pickled.

I like to add garlic to many of my vegetables, and it is now recommended that you acidify all garlic before using it in vegetables and oils. You can do this by peeling the cloves, scoring or mashing them, and covering them with vinegar for

twenty-four hours. Then remove the cloves and use them as you wish. Do not throw out the vinegar because it is flavored nicely and will make a nice vinaigrette.

Before preserving vegetables please read the information on food spoilage (page 10).

40

Vegetables	How to Prepare	Processing Time (10 lbs pressure)	
		Pint	Quart
		minutes	
Artichokes	Use small artichokes. Trim to 1¼ to 2 inches in length. Pre-cook 5 minutes in water to which ¾ cup of vinegar per gallon has been added. Drain. Pack hot into hot jars. Do not overfill. Cover with a boiling brine prepared by adding ¾ cup vinegar or lemon juice and 3 tablespoons salt to 1 gallon water. Fill to within ¾ inch of tops of pint or quart jars. Seal.	25	25
Asparagus	Sort, wash, and cut in lengths ¾ inch shorter than the jar or cut into 1- or 2-inch pieces. Cut off scales (bracts). Pre-cook in boiling water for 1 to 3 minutes to wilt. Then plunge quickly into cold water.		
	To pack whole: Gather a bundle of stalks with the ends down and fill jar. Do not pack tightly. Add ½ teaspoon salt for pints, 1 teaspoon salt for quarts. Cover with boiling water to ¾ inch of top of jar. Seal.	28	32
	To pack cuts: Fill to ¾ inch from top of jar with cuts. Add ½ teaspoon salt for pints, 1 teaspoon salt for quarts. Cover with boiling water to within ¾ inch of top of jar. Seal.	28	32
Beans, dried	*To pack hot:* Use any dried beans or peas. Soak in cold water for 12 to 18 hours in a cool place. Bring to a boil and boil 30 minutes. Pack into hot jars, leaving 1 inch headspace. Add ½ teaspoon salt to pints, 1 teaspoon to quarts. Cover with boiling water to 1 inch of top. Seal.	75	90
Beans, fresh lima	*To pack hot:* Proceed as directed for peas. Process as directed for lima beans. *To pack raw:* Use ½ teaspoon salt for pint jars; 1 teaspoon salt for quart jars. *Small beans:* Pack pint jars loosely to within 1 inch of tops; quarts to 1¼ inches. *Large beans:* Pack pint jars loosely to within ¾ inch of tops; quarts to 1¼ inches. Add salt. Fill to ¾ inch of top with boiling water. Seal.	40	50
Beans, string	Sort and snip or string if necessary. Use ½ teaspoon salt for pint jars; 1 teaspoon salt for quart jars. *To pack hot:* Cut in 1- to 1½-inch lengths. Pre-cook in boiling water until pliable, about 2 to 5 minutes. Pack hot into hot jars. Add salt. Cover to within ¾ inch of jar tops with the boiling liquid in which the beans were pre-cooked. Add boiling water if needed. Seal.	20	25
	If beans are left whole, pack beans standing on ends. Seal.	25	30
	To pack raw: Cut into 1-inch pieces. Pack tightly to within ¾ inch of jar tops. Add salt. Cover with boiling water to within ¾ inch of top. Seal.	20	25
Beets	*To pack hot:* Leave on roots and 1 to 1½ inch of stems. Boil until skin slips off (about 15 minutes). Dip in cold water. Peel, trim, and slice. Discard woody beets. Reheat in small amount of water. Pack hot into hot jars. Add ½ teaspoon salt to pint jars; 1 teaspoon salt to quart jars. Cover to within ½ inch of jar tops with the boiling liquid in which the beets were reheated. Add boiling water if needed. Seal.	35	40
	Raw packing of beets is not recommended.		

Vegetables	How to Prepare	Processing Time (10 lbs pressure)	
		Pint	Quart
Carrots	*To pack raw:* Wash and scrape or peel. Pack cold, sliced, or asparagus style to within 1 inch of tops of pint or quart jars. Add 1 teaspoon salt to pint jars; 1 teaspoon salt to quart jars. Add boiling water to within ¾ inch of top. Seal.	30	30
Celery	Prepare and slice. Use ½ teaspoon salt for pint jars; 1 teaspoon salt for quart jars.		
	To pack hot: Pre-cook 1 to 3 minutes depending on size and tenderness. Pack hot into hot jars. Add salt. Cover to within ¾ inch of jar tops with boiling liquid in which the celery was pre-cooked. Add boiling water if needed. Seal.	35	35
	To pack raw: Slice or cut asparagus style. Pack loosely to within ¾ inch of jar tops. Add salt. Cover with boiling water to within ¾ inch of tops. Seal.	30	30
Corn, whole kernel	*To pack hot:* Preserve very soon after harvest. Use a sharp knife to cut raw corn from cob to two-thirds of the total depth of the kernels. Do not scrape the cobs. Cover well with brine (1 level tablespoon salt to 1 quart water). Heat to boiling point. Pack hot into hot jars to within 1 inch of jar tops. Seal. Raw pack is not recommended.	55	70
Greens	Spinach, swiss chard, beet greens, other greens. Home preserving is not recommended.		
Mushrooms	NOTE: Trim stems and discolored parts. Rinse in cold water. Leave small mushrooms whole; cut larger ones into halves or quarters. Blanch in simmering hot water or steam for 4 minutes. Pack hot mushrooms into hot jars. Add ½ teaspoon salt and ½ teaspoon of lemon juice to pints. Add boiling cooking liquid or water to cover mushrooms, leaving ½ inch headspace. Mushrooms will be over-cooked if processed long enough to be safe. Apply lids and ring bands.	30	Don't use
Okra	*To pack hot:* Use young, tender pods. Wash and trim. Leave pods whole or cut into 1-inch pieces. Boil for 1 minute. Pack hot into hot jars, leaving 1 inch headspace. Add ½ teaspoon salt to pints, 1 teaspoon to quarts. Add boiling water to 1 inch to top. Seal.	25	40
Onions, small white	Follow directions for artichokes.		
Peas, fresh green	*To pack hot:* Can only young, tender peas. Hull and pre-cook for 1 to 4 minutes in a small amount of water until the skins wrinkle. Pack hot into hot jars to within 1¼ inches of tops. Add salt. Cover to within 1 inch of jar tops with the boiling liquid in which the peas were cooked. Add boiling water if needed. Seal.	40	45
	To pack raw: Pack loosely to within 1 inch of jar tops. Add ½ teaspoon salt for pint jars; 1 teaspoon salt for quart jars. Cover with boiling water to within 1 inch of top. Seal.	40	45
Peas, fresh black-eyed	*To pack hot:* Follow directions for green peas. Raw pack is not recommended.	50	55
Peppers, bell-green, red, and pimento	*To pack hot:* Cut out the stem end of each pepper, and remove the core and seeds. Peel peppers by heating in a gas flame or roasting in a very hot oven until the skins separate. Chill at once in cold water. Pack into jars. Cover with boiling water to within ½ inch of jar tops. Add ½ teaspoon salt to pint jars; 1 teaspoon salt to quart jars. It is also necessary to add 1½ teaspoons bottled lemon juice to pint jars; 1 tablespoon lemon juice to each quart jar. (Process at only 5 pounds pressure; higher pressures affect texture and flavor.) Seal.	(5 lb pressure) 50	60

Vegetables	How to Prepare	Processing Time (10 lbs pressure)	
		Pint	Quart
		minutes	
Potatoes, new	Peel new potatoes. Leave small ones whole; cut larger ones in halves. Pack cold without pre-cooking. Add boiling brine made with 1½ to 2 tablespoons salt to 1 quart water. Fill to within ¾ to 1 inch of jar tops. Seal.	35	40
Potatoes, sweet	Wash and remove any blemishes. *To pack dry:* Place in steamer over boiling water or boil in a small amount of water until crisp-tender. Peel and cut into pieces. Pack tightly into jars, pressing to fill spaces. Add no salt or liquid. Apply lids and ring bands.	65	95
	To pack wet: Steam or boil as for dry pack, but remove as soon as skins slip off easily. Peel, cut into pieces, and pack hot into jars to within 1 inch of tops. Add ½ teaspoon salt to quarts. Cover with boiling water or a syrup of 1 part sugar to 2 parts water, leaving ¾-inch headspace. Apply lids and ring bands.	55	90
Pumpkin or mature squash, cubed	*To pack hot:* Wash, remove seeds, and peel. Cut into 1-inch cubes. Add enough water to cover; bring to a boil. Pack hot cubes to ½ inch of the top. Add ½ teaspoon salt to pints; 1 teaspoon to quarts. Cover with hot cooking liquid, leaving ½-inch headspace. Seal. Raw pack is not recommended.	55	90
Pumpkin or mature squash, strained	Scrape out fibrous material and cut flesh and rind into strips. Boil in water, or steam, until flesh is soft. Scrape flesh from rind and press through a colander. Bring to a boil. Pack hot into hot jars to within ¾ to 1 inch of tops. Add ½ teaspoon salt to pint jars; 1 teaspoon salt to quart jars. Seal. Raw pack is not recommended.	85	115
Squash, summer crookneck, zucchini, pattypan	Preserving summer squash produces a soft to mushy product. Wash and trim ends; do not peel. Cut into ½-inch thick slices. *To pack hot:* Put into a pan, add water to just cover, and bring to boil. Pack hot into hot jars, filling loosely up to jar shoulders. Add ½ teaspoon salt to pints, 1 teaspoon to quarts. Cover with boiling cooking liquid, leaving ½-inch headspace. Apply lids and ring bands.	30	40
	To pack raw: Pack slices tightly into jars to within 1 inch of tops. Add salt for hot pack, then fill jars with boiling water, leaving ½-inch head space. Apply lids and ring bands.	25	30
Turnips	Follow directions for carrots.		

42

	Processing Time (minutes) at Altitudes		
*Product**	**Less than 3,000 feet**	**3,000 to 7,000 feet**	**Over 7,000 feet**
Asparagus	15	25	35
Beans, lima	30	60	85
Beans, snap or wax	15	30	45
Beets, whole or sliced	15	30	45
Carrots	15	30	45
Corn, whole kernel	50	90	135
Mushrooms	20	40	60
Okra	15	30	45
Parsnips	15	30	45
Peas, green	30	60	85
Peas, black-eye	30	60	85
Potatoes, new-whole	20	40	60
Rutabagas, sliced or diced	30	60	85
Squash, cubed	20	40	60
Sweet potatoes	50	90	135
Turnips, cubed	15	30	45

Processing Times at 15 Pounds per Square Inch at Various Altitudes for Pint and Quart Mason Jars Processed in 12-, 16-, or 21-Quart Pressure Devices (Hot or Cold Pack Procedure).

*Processing times at 15 pounds per square inch have not been established for all vegetables.

43

© Steven Mark Needham/Envision

44

Artichoke Hearts

Every year we vacation in Carmel, California, and get pounds of baby artichokes from a little town on its outskirts called Castroville. I like to put lots of these up because I use them in so many recipes. They are very expensive if you buy them in jars or frozen, so it pays to put them up.

Artichoke hearts	White wine vinegar
Water	Salt to taste

Pick out small artichokes and trim to 1½ to 2 inches long. Remove the dark, tough outer leaves. Cook until tender in enough water to cover, adding ¾ cup white wine vinegar per gallon of water. Drain. Make a brine of 1 gallon of water, adding 3 tablespoons salt and ¾ cup white wine vinegar. Bring to a boil. Fill hot jars with artichoke hearts and add boiling brine to within ¾ inch of the top of the jar. Release air bubbles, clean rims, and seal. Process in a pressure device for 25 minutes at 10 pounds pressure for a pint jar. You will need 10 to 12 artichokes per pint jar.

Artichoke Canapes

This is a simple appetizer that is very tasty.

This mixture can be put into an ovenproof dish and baked at 400°F, covered, for 30 to 35 minutes. Serve it with bread or crackers, or hollow out a round French bread and fill it with the mixture. Wrap the filled bread in foil and bake for 30 to 35 minutes. Serve it with the bread you removed to hollow it out.

8 ounces Artichoke Hearts
¾ cup mayonnaise
2 tablespoons olive oil
1½ teaspoons Italian herbs
2 cloves garlic, minced
¾ teaspoon salt
1 teaspoon pepper
1 cup Parmesan cheese
¼ cup whipped cream
  cheese with chives
French baguette

Preheat oven to 400°F.

Blend all ingredients except baguette in a food processor with a metal blade. Slice bread thinly and put about 1 tablespoon of the mixture on each slice, mounding it slightly. Cook in a 400°F oven for 8 to 10 minutes or until golden on top.

Chicken Scallopini with Artichokes

I use six whole chicken breasts for this recipe. It depends how much else you serve with them, but my family always eats two half-breasts each.

6 whole chicken breasts
1 pint Artichoke Hearts
1½ cups flour
1½ teaspoons garlic powder

1½ teaspoons garlic salt
3 teaspoons pepper
1½ tablespoons chicken soup base
1 tablespoon tarragon
Olive oil for frying
4 tablespoons butter
¼ cup green onions, chopped
¼ cup chicken broth
½ cup vermouth
½ cup cream

Preheat oven to 300°F.

Bone, skin, and flatten chicken breasts and put in ice water. Drain Artichoke Hearts and set aside. Mix flour, garlic powder, garlic salt, pepper, chicken soup base, and tarragon. Dredge chicken in flour mixture, and fry in oil in a large frying pan. As soon as the chicken is nicely browned, remove it and drain on paper towels. Continue until all chicken is cooked. When all chicken is done, put on a cookie sheet and keep it warm in a 300°F oven while you make the sauce.

Pour oil out of pan and add butter to pan, scraping the pan as the butter melts to deglaze it. Add the scallions and sauté for 2 minutes. Add chicken broth and vermouth and cook, stirring, for 2 more minutes. Add cream. Blend well and add artichokes. Cook 2 to 3 minutes more. Put chicken on a serving platter and spoon sauce and artichokes over the chicken. Serves 6 to 12.

Miniature Tangy Crepes

These crepes can be made ahead of time and frozen. You can also assemble them up to an hour before you need them.

Crepes:
2 eggs
¼ teaspoon salt

½ teaspoon parsley
½ teaspoon tarragon
½ teaspoon fine herbs
1 cup milk
2 tablespoons butter, melted
Vegetable oil for cooking crepes

Filling:
½ cup sour cream
2 tablespoons vermouth
2 teaspoons tarragon
3 tablespoons Dijon mustard
1½ teaspoons lemon pepper
1 egg yolk
1 quart Herbed Asparagus,
    cut to fit crepes

Mix all the ingredients for the crepes in a blender. Refrigerate for at least 1 hour. When ready to make, use a fry pan rubbed with oil. Put 1 tablespoon of batter in a hot frying pan and cook until bubbles form. Turn over and cook until golden. You can make a couple at a time because you only make them 3 or 4 inches round. Use what you need and freeze the rest.

Make the mustard filling by heating the sour cream, vermouth, tarragon, mustard, and lemon pepper in a saucepan until hot. In a separate bowl, beat the egg yolk and a couple spoonfuls of the sauce. Blend well and add to the rest of the sauce. Heat slowly, stirring until thickened. Let cool.

Put 1½ teaspoons of sauce on each crepe with 1 piece of asparagus, and roll up.

Serve on a pretty platter. Can be refrigerated for 1 hour. Makes approximately 24 crepes.

45

Herbed Asparagus

This asparagus is so good. Use it on your favorite salad, or in a quiche or a wonderful tangy crepe.

28 pounds asparagus
1 quart water
3 quarts white wine vinegar
2 tablespoons sugar

Per quart:
½ teaspoon salt

¼ teaspoon pepper
⅛ teaspoon fine herbs
½ teaspoon tarragon
¼ cup olive oil
¼ teaspoon celery seed

Clean asparagus and cut to fit in quart jar. Scrape ends with vegetable peeler, and blanch in boiling water. Drain. Bring water, vinegar, and sugar just to a boil and then turn heat down so it stays hot. Put salt, pepper, fine herbs, tarragon, oil, and celery seed in each hot quart jar. Fill jars with asparagus and pour in hot vinegar mixture. Release air bubbles, clean rims, and seal with hot lids. Process in a hot water bath for 30 minutes. Makes 14 quarts.

Asparagus Quiche

Quiches are quick to make and delicious. They are a great way to use leftovers and have something everyone will love.

1¼ cups flour
½ cup Crisco
½ teaspoon salt
2½ tablepoons ice water
2 tablespoons unsalted butter
1 onion, diced
¼ pound ham, diced
1 pint Herbed Asparagus, drained and diced
1 cup Swiss cheese, grated
3 eggs
2 cups whipping cream
½ teaspoon salt
¾ teaspoon pepper
Pinch of nutmeg

Preheat oven to 425°F.

Mix flour, Crisco, and salt, rubbing the fat and flour until it is broken into pieces that are pea size. Add water and mix until it just forms a ball. Roll it out to ⅛-inch thickness and place in a greased 10-inch pie plate. Flute the edges. Partially cook the shell in a 425°F oven for 7 or 8 minutes. Remove from the oven.

Reduce oven to 375°F.

Melt butter in a small skillet and sauté onions for 2 minutes, then add ham and cook 2 more minutes. Spoon mixture into pie shell. Sprinkle the asparagus and cheese over the ham.

Mix eggs, cream, salt, pepper, and nutmeg in a blender. Pour over the pie filling and bake in a 375°F oven for 25 to 30 minutes or until quiche is puffed and browned. Serves 8.

© Fredric Stein/FPG International

This Asparagus Quiche makes a beautiful luncheon dish or first course.

Composed Tuna Salad

Use a dinner-size plate for this salad. I love to serve this with large hot popovers.

Bibb lettuce
Red leaf lettuce
Romaine lettuce
Tuna (packed in water)
Carrots, julienned
Celery, julienned
Jicama, julienned
Zucchini, julienned
1 quart Herbed Asparagus
Tomatoes stuffed with Devilish Egg Filling (see page 52)
Three-Pepper Terrine (see page 47)

Dressing:
½ cup preserving liquid from Herbed Asparagus
¾ cup Lemon-Thyme Oil (see page 64)
½ cup vinegar
1 teaspoon salt
1 teaspoon pepper
1 teaspoon Raspberry Mustard (see page 68)
1 teaspoon thyme
1 garlic clove

Mix all lettuces together and divide among dinner plates. Arrange about ¼ cup tuna in the center of each plate on the lettuce. Mix the jullienned vegetables together and arrange them around the mounds of tuna. Divide the asparagus among the plates, curving them on one side of the julienned vegetables. Put a few stuffed tomatoes on each plate. Carefully slice the Three-Pepper Terrine and lay it opposite the asparagus on the other side of the plate.

Mix all ingredients for the dressing in a blender and drizzle over salads.

46

Three-Color Peppers

Peppers are available most of the year, but it is so convenient to have them on hand.

12 peppers: 4 yellow, 4 red, 4 green   **2 teaspoons salt**
                                                 6 teaspoons lemon juice

Place peppers on a cookie sheet in hot oven (450°F) until skins blister. Remove them from the oven and put them in a plastic bag for about 10 minutes. Remove and rub skin off. Cut peppers in half and remove seeds, then cut into strips. Put ½ teaspoon salt and 1½ teaspoons lemon juice in each of 4 pint jars. Add peppers to jars and cover with boiling water. Leave ½-inch headspace. Release air bubbles, clean rims, and seal. Process in a pressure device at 5 pounds for 50 minutes. Makes 4 pints.

© Burke/Triolo

Three-Pepper Soup

I like to combine this soup with creamy spinach soup. Pour them at the same time from opposite sides of the bowl and they will stay separate.

2 tablespoons olive oil
2 pints Three-Color Peppers, diced
¼ cup onion, chopped
1 quart tomatoes, chopped
5 basil leaves, chopped
1 tablespoon chicken soup base
2 cups chicken broth
Salt to taste
Pepper to taste
½ cup cream

Put olive oil in a soup kettle and sauté peppers and onions for 3 minutes. Add all other ingredients except cream. Cook for 30 minutes. Cool slightly. Put in blender in batches and purée. Return to pan and stir in cream. Heat thoroughly. Serves 8.

Three-Pepper Terrine

This terrine is a beautiful mixture of colors. It is wonderful to serve alongside your favorite salad or as an appetizer.

1½ pints Three-Color Peppers
4½ tablespoons olive oil
1 onion, minced
3 garlic cloves, minced
¼ pound mushrooms, diced
1 teaspoon oregano
1 teaspoon pepper
1½ teaspoons salt
½ cup Parmesan cheese
1½ cups Monterey Jack cheese
4 eggs, beaten

Preheat oven to 375°F.

Drain peppers and dice. Put oil in a skillet and add onion, garlic, mushrooms, and peppers. Sauté for 3 to 4 minutes. Put in a bowl and add oregano, pepper, salt, and Parmesan and Jack cheeses. Mix well and stir in beaten eggs.

Put the mixture into a 9 x 13-inch loaf pan that has been sprayed with a vegetable-oil spray. Press the mixture down with the back of a spoon and smooth. Cook for 40 to 50 minutes or until golden brown. Remove from oven and let cool in pan for 15 minutes. Loosen terrine on sides with a knife and turn out onto a plate. Cover and refrigerate until ready to use. Can be made up to 2 days ahead. Serves 12.

Three-Pepper Pasta Salad

Noodles seem to really soak up dressing, so if you make this salad in the morning or the day before, taste it and add more of what it needs.

10 ounces dry pasta or
   12 ounces fresh
6 tablespoons light olive oil
8 ounces Three-Color Peppers
2 carrots, diced small
2 celery stalks, diced small
4 green onions, chopped
2 large tomatoes, seeded and diced
2 teaspoons lemon pepper
1 teaspoon dried tarragon or
   1 tablespoon fresh, minced
1 teaspoon salt
¼ cup tarragon vinegar

48

Cook pasta in salted water with 2 tablespoons of oil. Drain and rinse in cold water to stop cooking. Put in bowl and toss with 1 tablespoon of oil; this will keep the pasta from sticking together while you fix the rest of the ingredients.

Add peppers, carrots, celery, scallions, and tomatoes. Toss well. Sprinkle with lemon pepper, tarragon, salt, vinegar, and the remaining olive oil. Toss and adjust seasonings to taste. Serves 10 to 12 as a side dish.

This Three-Pepper Pasta Salad is full of color and flavor.

Sweet-and-Sour Beans

These beans are tasty served plain on your favorite salad, or they can be heated for a tangy side dish.

3 pounds green beans	3 cups rice vinegar
⅓ cup olive oil	¾ cup sugar
1 large onion, minced	3 teaspoons celery salt
2 garlic cloves, minced	1 teaspoon pepper
4 cups water	2 teaspoons salt

Cut ends off beans and cut into 1-inch pieces. Cook in salted water just until tender, about 6 minutes. Heat oil and sauté onion and garlic until tender. Add the rest of the ingredients to the oil, except the beans. Stir until the sugar is dissolved and bring the mixture to a boil. Add the beans and boil 2 minutes. Ladle into hot jars, packing tightly, release air bubbles, clean rims, and seal with hot lids. Process in a hot water bath for 10 minutes. Makes 5 pints.

© Dan Wilby

Bean Torta

I love torta made out of any vegetable. Torta can be served hot or cold.

½ teaspoon salt
3 zucchini, shredded
1 pint Sweet-and-Sour Beans
1½ cups cheddar cheese, shredded
½ cup Parmesan cheese, grated
1 teaspoon oregano
1½ teaspoons cracked black pepper
⅓ cup olive oil
4 eggs, beaten

Preheat oven to 350°F.

Put salt on zucchini and toss. Let drain in a colander for 30 minutes. Rinse off salt and dry. Combine zucchini, beans, cheddar cheese, Parmesan cheese, oregano, pepper, olive oil, and eggs. Mix well and place in a greased 9 x 13-inch pan. Cook at 350°F for 40 to 45 minutes or until nice and brown. Cut into squares to serve. Serves 12.

Mixed-Bean Salad

Use this recipe next time you have to bring a salad to a potluck dinner.

1 quart Sweet-and-Sour Beans (reserve liquid)
1 15½-ounce can kidney beans
1 15½-ounce can garbanzo beans
1 head iceberg lettuce, shredded
1 red pepper, diced small
2 celery stalks, diced small

Dressing:
Reserved liquid from beans
¾ cup mayonnaise
¼ cup chili sauce
1 teaspoon salt
Crushed tortilla chips
Fried bacon, crushed

Mix salad ingredients in a large bowl. Mix first 4 dressing ingredients together in a blender. Toss salad with dressing. Sprinkle with tortilla chips and bacon, toss, and serve. Serves 12.

49

© Dan Wilby

These Sweet-and-Sour Beans are so quick and colorful that they will do justice to any main dish.

CHAPTER 4
PICKLES, CHUTNEYS, & RELISHES

By adding vinegar, sugar, salt, and seasonings to your vegetables you can create

pickles, chutneys, or relishes, all of which will add interest to your cooking. You

can adjust the seasonings from mild to pungent, according to your taste.

You will not need any new equipment for pickling other than what you have for

preserving. Just make sure you use glass, enamel, plastic, or stainless steel utensils

because the brine will react with other metals.

Pickles, relishes, and chutneys are all processed in a hot water bath. This is to assure

a seal and will not affect the texture of your pickles.

You can put up all sorts of vegetables in pickling liquid. The most common vegetable

is the cucumber, but I also love pickling many other vegetables. I have included

recipes for beans and asparagus just to give you a few ideas. Chutneys are also made

with the addition of vinegar and may be a mixture of fruits and vegetables with spices. Chutneys may be served as a condiment with other foods, but they are also great used in many recipes as a main ingredient, which you will see in the recipes that follow the chutneys.

Relishes also use pickling methods and ingredients. Relishes are usually ground fruit and vegetables, blended with vinegar and spices for a more piquant flavor.

52

© Gary Buss/FPG International

Linda's Sweet Pickles

These pickles make Devilish Eggs taste extra special. Try them also in a special Red-Potato Salad.

**4 pounds pickling cucumbers
(Kirbies)
½ cup pickling salt
2 medium onions, minced
¼ cup red pepper, minced
2 teaspoons celery salt**

**1 teaspoon dry mustard
1 teaspoon pepper
3 cups apple cider vinegar
3 cups sugar
3 tablespoons pickling spice**

Slice cucumbers about ½ inch thick and put in a large enamel or stainless steel bowl. Add salt and cover with cold water. Add ice cubes to cover surface. Let sit 12 hours replacing ice 2 or 3 times. Drain pickles and rinse well in cold water. Put all the rest of the ingredients into a pan and bring to a boil. Add the cucumbers and return to a boil again. Remove from heat and fill hot jars with pickles and vinegar mixture. Be sure to pack pickles tightly. Release air bubbles, clean rims, and seal with hot lids. Process in a hot water bath for 10 minutes. Makes 5 pints.

Devilish Eggs

Almost everyone I know loves deviled eggs. They are so easy and can be topped with so many good things.

**8 eggs
2 tablespoons onion, minced
2 tablespoons mayonnaise
2 tablespoons celery, chopped
2 tablespoons Linda's Sweet
   Pickles, minced
1 tablespoon cream cheese
1½ teaspoons mustard
½ teaspoon celery salt
1½ teaspoons lemon pepper
¾ teaspoon salt
Cooked baby shrimp, crab, caviar,
   smoked salmon, crumbled crisp
   bacon, avocado pieces, or asparagus
   tips (optional)**

Boil eggs and put in ice water to cool. When cool, peel eggs and cut in half. Remove the yolks, setting the whites aside. Put yolks and all other ingredients, except optional toppings, into a food processor fitted with a metal blade. Process until just blended, adding more lemon pepper if necessary. Put egg mixture into a pastry bag and squeeze into egg white. Top if desired. Makes 16.

This potato salad would be wonderful for a picnic. Just make sure you keep it cold, since it is made with mayonnaise and sour cream.

Red-Potato Salad

I like to use small red potatoes. I am very fond of the vinaigrette potato salads everyone serves today, but sometimes the old heavy mayonnaise potato salad can't be beat. I like to top my salad with hot crisp bacon right before I serve it.

2½ pounds small red potatoes
⅓ cup Linda's Sweet Pickles
⅓ cup red onion, diced
⅓ cup celery, diced
4 hard-boiled eggs, chopped coarsely
2 tablespoons fresh parsley, minced
1 cup mayonnaise
¼ cup sour cream
¾ cup celery seed
2 teaspoons mustard
3 tablespoons vinegar
Salt to taste
Freshly ground black pepper to taste

Boil potatoes until just tender. Drain and let sit until cold. Peel and dice potatoes and add pickles, red onion, celery, eggs, and parsley.

Mix together mayonnaise, sour cream, celery seed, mustard, vinegar, salt, and pepper. Pour dressing on potatoes and toss until all potatoes are coated with dressing. Refrigerate until used. Serves 6 to 8.

Apple-Tomato Chutney

This is a sweet tomato chutney. Try it with Pork Tenderloin or on Stuffed Chicken Breasts.

4 pounds tomatoes	2 cups rice vinegar
2 pounds apples	3 cups sugar
2 tablespoons lemon juice	¼ teaspoon mace
1 large onion, chopped	1 teaspoon basil
1 tablespoon olive oil	½ teaspoon turmeric

Drop a few tomatoes at a time in boiling water for 30 seconds, then peel. Dice the tomatoes and let them drain while you do the other preparation. Peel, core, and mince the apples and add lemon juice. Sauté chopped onion in the olive oil in a large saucepan until transparent. Add the tomatoes, apples, and the rest of the ingredients to the saucepan. Cook at a soft boil for 20 to 30 minutes until fruit is tender and mixture is thickened. Ladle into hot jars, clean rims, and seal with hot lids. Process in a hot water bath for 10 minutes. Makes 7 half-pint jars.

54

© Dan Wilby

Making this chutney is a wonderful way to use abundant apple and tomato crops.

Pork Tenderloin

When a tenderloin is cooked correctly it is tender and delicious, so do not over-cook.

1 pork tenderloin, 1½ to 2 pounds
2 garlic cloves, minced
Salt to taste
Pepper to taste
1 teaspoon rosemary
8 ounces Apple-Tomato Chutney

Preheat oven to 425°F.

Pat tenderloin dry with paper towels. Rub garlic on all sides of meat. Sprinkle with salt, pepper, and rosemary. Bake for 10 minutes then turn oven down to 350°F and continue cooking for 35 more minutes. Warm chutney in saucepan. Remove tenderloin and slice thin. Put a tablespoon of chutney on each plate with a few slices of pork. Serves 3 to 4.

Stuffed Chicken Breasts

This is a terrific dish for a dinner party.

6 chicken breasts
2 tablespoons unsalted butter
2 tablespoons onion, minced
2 tablespoons celery, minced
2 tablespoons carrot, minced
½ cup long grain and wild rice mix
1½ cups chicken broth
1 teaspoon onion salt
1 tablespoon olive oil
1 cup Apple-Tomato Chutney

Preheat oven to 400°F.

Skin and bone breasts and pound flat. Put 1 tablespoon butter in a saucepan. Melt butter and add onion, celery, and carrots. Sauté until onions are transparent. Pour in rice and broth and bring to a boil, then simmer, covered, for 20 to 25 minutes. Remove from heat and toss with onion salt. Take 1 chicken breast and put about ¼ cup rice mixture on chicken. Roll breast up and tie with a piece of string. Continue with each breast. Heat 1 tablespoon butter and the olive oil in a sauté pan until hot. Brown chicken over high heat just for color. When browned put chicken into a 9-inch square baking dish and pour Apple-Tomato Chutney over the chicken. Bake for 25 to 30 minutes. Spoon some of the hot chutney on each piece of chicken and serve. This is good served with a vinaigrette salad. Serves 6.

Turkey-Cranberry Sandwich in a Pita

What is Thanksgiving without leftover turkey! This pita sandwich is a delicious and different way to enjoy your turkey.

1 pita bread
1½ tablespoons mayonnaise
1½ tablespoons Cranberry-Lemon Relish
4 slices turkey
3 thin slices red onion
2 slices provolone cheese
2 thin slices tomato, diced small
1 piece red leaf lettuce, shredded
2 teaspoons pecans, chopped

Take pita and cut top 1½ inches off. Mix mayonnaise and relish together and spread inside pita. Carefully stack turkey, red onion, and cheese in pita and sprinkle in tomato, lettuce, and chopped pecans. Makes 1 sandwich.

© Dan Wilby

This pita sandwich would be great in a boxed lunch.

55

Cranberry-Lemon Relish

I love this relish so much that I eat it plain. It is really good with turkey and chicken and wonderful in sandwiches.

12 ounces fresh cranberries	¾ cup sugar
Juice from 2 lemons, zest reserved	¼ cup walnuts, chopped fine
½ cup water	1 tablespoon Grand Marnier

Swirl cranberries in a food processor or blender to coarsely chop. Put into a saucepan. Remove the zest from the lemons and add it, lemon juice, and water to the cranberries. Add sugar and blend over medium heat until sugar dissolves. Cook 5 minutes. Add walnuts and Grand Marnier and cook 2 minutes more. Ladle into hot jars, wipe rims, and seal with hot lids. Process in hot water bath for 10 minutes. Makes 3 half-pint jars.

© Dan Wilby

Pepper and Onion Relish complements many foods, so you can be creative with it.

56

Pepper and Onion Relish

This relish is a beautiful color. It gives chicken a lovely sweet and tangy taste.

1 large onion, minced
2 tablespoons olive oil
2 large green bell peppers
½ cup canned chilies, drained and diced
1½ cups cider vinegar
6 cups sugar
6 ounces liquid pectin

Sauté onion in oil until transparent. Grind peppers and chilies together, then add to the onion. Add vinegar and sugar, stirring until sugar is dissolved. Bring to a full rolling boil. Add pectin and return to a full boil and boil 1 minute. Skim off any foam that forms and ladle into hot jars. Clean rims, and seal with hot lids. Makes 8 half-pint jars.

Chicken Cooked in a Whiskey-Pepper Sauce

You can use this sauce with any fowl, but it has a strong flavor so use sparingly.

1 3½- to 4-pound whole chicken
2 tablespoons butter
Salt to taste
Pepper to taste
¾ cup Pepper and Onion Relish
2 tablespoons whiskey
1 garlic clove, minced
½ teaspoon pepper
1 teaspoon salt
½ teaspoon cumin
1 ounce slivered almonds

Preheat oven to 350°F.

Rub chicken with butter and sprinkle with salt and pepper. Roast chicken in oven for 1 hour. Make the sauce by putting all other ingredients, except almonds, in a saucepan and heat through. After the chicken has cooked for an hour, turn the oven up to 400°F. Baste with the sauce every 5 minutes for 10 minutes or until the bird is nicely browned. Heat the sauce again and add the almonds. Put some sauce on the platter, quarter the chicken, and lay on the sauce. Makes 1 cup sauce. Chicken serves 4.

Grilled Lamb with Peppermint Sauce

I use this sauce with all cuts of lamb. If you use it with a boned leg of lamb, double the recipe so you have plenty of sauce.

⅓ cup Pepper and Onion Relish
2 tablespoons vermouth
1 teaspoon crème de menthe
1 teaspoon dried mint leaves, crushed
1 teaspoon salt
½ teaspoon pepper
4 lambchops
Fresh mint leaves (for garnish)

For sauce, mix first 6 ingredients and heat until relish liquefies. Grill lamb over hot coals. When meat is almost done, brush each side once or twice with the sauce. Do not overcook; the meat should take 12 to 15 minutes per side depending on desired doneness. Reheat the remaining sauce and pour on a plate. Put the lamb on the plate and turn the meat over once to cover with the sauce.

Serve with fresh mint leaves and a tomato rose garnishing the plate. Makes ½ cup sauce. Serves 6.

Halibut with Pepper-Cream Sauce

This sauce is so beautiful. One way to show this dish is to serve it on a white plate.

½ cup Pepper and Onion Relish
⅓ cup diced celery
⅓ cup diced tomato
1 teaspoon dill
1 tablespoon lemon juice
¼ cup cream
1 teaspoon cornstarch
1 tablespoon vegetable oil
4 6-ounce halibut fillets

To make sauce, combine first 5 ingredients. Warm sauce to liquefy relish. Add cream and stir. Mix together cornstarch and ¼ cup cold water. When combined, blend into sauce. Heat just until the sauce slightly thickens. Brush oil on fillets and grill over hot coals, 3 minutes per side. Pour a small amount of sauce on serving plate. Place halibut fillet on top of sauce and spoon sauce across the center of the halibut. Makes about 1¼ cups sauce; enough for 4 servings.

57

This beautiful halibut dish is sure to become one of your all-time favorites.

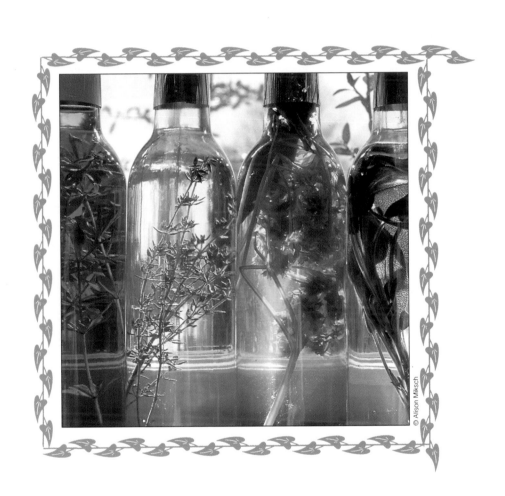

CHAPTER 5

VINEGARS, MUSTARDS, & OILS

One of the many wonderful things about putting up foods is the joy of giving these treasures to your friends. Nothing is more appreciated than a handmade gift. Buying a great basket and filling it with peach-nut bread in a new loaf pan tied with a ribbon, peach butter, and a beautiful crystal jar to serve the peach butter in makes an unforgettable gift.

Another fun gift idea is the vinegar, mustard, and oil recipes I have included in this section. You can put these in beautiful and interesting bottles, making the containers themselves a special gift. Get into the giving spirit and share your cooking talent with others. You'll be surprised how much they will value such a gift.

Raspberry Sauce

I love having Raspberry Sauce on hand. It makes so many desserts special by just drizzling some on each plate. Make cheesecake and set it in a pool of this sauce. It also makes a wonderful Raspberry-Chive Butter for pan-fried fish and a light Raspberry Sabayon.

12 baskets red raspberries	1 cup honey
1 teaspoon gelatin	2 cups sugar
2 tablespoons Grand Marnier	2 tablespoons lemon juice

Crush raspberries and remove seeds using either a fine mesh sieve or a food processor. Dissolve the gelatin and Grand Marnier in a cup set in a pan of boiling water. Set aside. Put raspberry purée in a large pan and add honey, sugar, and lemon juice. Stir to dissolve sugar and bring to a boil. Slow boil for 5 minutes. Add dissolved gelatin and mix well. Ladle into hot jars, clean rims, and seal with hot lids. Process in hot water bath for 10 minutes. Makes 7 half-pint jars.

60

© Alison Miksch

Raspberry Sabayon

This is a light, elegant dessert that must be prepared right before serving. Serve it in your finest crystal glasses with some ladyfingers or lace cookies on the side.

3 eggs, separated
⅓ cup sugar
2 teaspoons lemon juice
½ cup Raspberry Sauce

Whip egg whites until stiff and set aside. Put egg yolks, sugar, and lemon juice in the top of a double boiler. With a wire whisk, whip until the yolks lighten and the mixture thickens; this will take about 5 minutes. When the mixture thickens add the Raspberry Sauce and continue whipping while cooking 3 minutes more. Remove from heat and whip in a large spoonful of the egg whites. When mixed, fold in the rest of the egg whites and completely blend. Serve immediately. Makes 4 to 5 servings.

Raspberry-Chive Butter

This is a tasty butter to use on any pan-fried or grilled fish. Substitute tarragon for the fish spice, and it is great for grilled chicken.

4 tablespoons butter, softened
2 tablespoons Raspberry Sauce
2 teaspoons chopped chives
½ teaspoon fish spice (or dill)

Mix all ingredients until creamy. Put a tablespoon on top of each piece of fish. Makes 6 tablespoons.

© Steven Mark Needham/Envision

Lemon Curd

Lemon Curd is marvelous to have on hand. It makes desserts easy to assemble. Curds must be made with high-acid fruits such as limes, oranges, pomegranates, or cranberries. Most fruits need a little extra acid, so add some lemon juice to all these fruits except for limes.

Zest of 4 lemons	1½ cups butter
1½ cups lemon juice	10 egg yolks
1¾ cups sugar	1 teaspoon vanilla

Put all ingredients into the top of a double boiler. The water should be just simmering so you don't overcook the eggs. Stirring constantly, cook until the mixture thickens. This will take 20 to 25 minutes. Ladle into hot jars, clean rims, and seal with hot lids. Makes 4 half-pint jars.

Lemon Chiffon Pie

This is a light and airy pie that takes no time to make when you have Lemon Curd on hand. The pie crust recipe is my grandmother's. She worked in a restaurant, making their pies. It was said people came from miles around just for her pie. This crust is light and flaky as long as you make sure you don't overwork it. I never make it in a food processor because that toughens it. Always use a fork or pastry blender to make it and handle it as little as possible.

61

2 cups flour
1 teaspoon salt
⅔ cup plus 2 tablespoons Crisco
5 tablespoons ice water
1½ cups whipping cream
1 cup sour cream
½ cup confectioner's sugar
1 teaspoon vanilla
8 ounces Lemon Curd

Preheat oven to 425°F.

Make crust by mixing the flour and salt and cutting in the Crisco. Add water and just blend. The less the dough is handled the flakier it will be. Roll out half the dough to fit a greased 9-inch pie plate. Flute edges and prick bottom of crust. Cook in a 425°F oven for 10 to 12 minutes. Roll out the other half of the dough to a disk 8¾ inches round. Prick the disk and cook it on a cookie sheet in a 425°F oven for 8 to 10 minutes. Cool. Put whipping cream and sour cream in a mixing bowl and refrigerate for 15 minutes. Whip the cream mixture until soft peaks form. Add powdered sugar and vanilla, beating until

stiff. Remove 1 cup of the cream mixture and set aside. Fold in the Lemon
Curd. Put 1½ cups of the lemon mixture into the pie shell. Cover with the
pastry disk. Top with remaining filling.
Garnish with the reserved cream and top
with a lemon rose. Serves 6 to 8.

Lemon Cheese Squares

Try this recipe using chocolate pudding
in place of the Lemon Curd.

1 cup flour
½ cup butter, softened
6 ounces cream cheese
8 ounces Lemon Curd
1 tablespoon sugar
2 cups whipping cream
1 teaspoon vanilla
1 teaspoon lemon extract
⅓ cup plus 1 tablespoon
    confectioner's sugar

Preheat oven to 350°F.

Mix flour and butter together and
press into a greased 9-inch square pan.
Bake for 10 minutes. Cool.

Beat cream cheese with half of the
Lemon Curd and the sugar until
smooth. Spread on cooled crust.

Whip cream, vanilla, lemon extract,
and confectioner's sugar until stiff.
Reserve 2 cups of whipped cream. Mix
remaining whipped cream with the last 4
ounces of lemon curd. Spread the
whipped cream and lemon curd mixture
over the cream cheese. Spread remaining whipped cream over top. Refrigerate
at least 3 hours before serving. Cut into
squares. Serves 8 to 10.

62

© Steven Mark Needham/Envision

Try using this Strawberry-Mint Vinegar in dressings or on cooked vegetables.

Strawberry-Mint Vinegar

This vinegar is a beautiful rosy color, so make sure you put it in pretty,
clear bottles to show it off. It has a nice fruity flavor and makes a
wonderful sauce for chicken.

4 cups strawberries, crushed   2 quarts rice vinegar
8 fresh mint leaves

Put the berries into a large glass container with a tight-fitting lid. Add
the mint leaves. Warm the vinegar and pour over the strawberries and
mint leaves. Cover tightly and store in a dark place. Remove the mint
leaves after 12 hours and discard. Continue storing for another 36
hours. After the 2 days have passed, strain the vinegar through 2 layers
of cheesecloth and pour into decorative bottles. Cork the bottles or
screw on tops tightly. Store the vinegar in a dark cool place, until ready
to use. Makes 2 quarts.

Chicken with Strawberry-Mint Vinegar Sauce

This is a wonderful chicken dish to serve at your next party.

8 large chicken breasts
1 cup flour
1 teaspoon salt
1 teaspoon pepper
1 tablespoon fried chicken spice
1 tablespoon tarragon
¼ cup vegetable oil
¾ cup butter
¼ cup minced green onion
½ teaspoon salt
½ teaspoon ground white pepper
½ cup Strawberry-Mint Vinegar
1 chicken bouillon cube
½ cup cream

Bone and skin chicken breasts and pound them between two pieces of wax paper until thin. Mix together flour, salt, pepper, chicken spice, and tarragon. Heat oil in heavy fry pan. When oil is hot, dip chicken in flour mixture. Fry a few pieces at a time until all are done. Remember that they are thin, so don't overcook. When all breasts are cooked, pour oil out of pan and add the butter. As butter melts, scrape the bits of chicken off the bottom of the pan. Add scallions and sauté 2 minutes. Add the salt, pepper, vinegar, and chicken bouillon cube. Stir well to dissolve the bouillon cube. Cook another 2 minutes. Add the cream and blend well. Put chicken on warm plate and drizzle with sauce. Garnish with a few fresh strawberries. Serves 8.

© Alison Miksch

63

Tangy Vegetables

You can add butter and flavored vinegar to many different vegetables.

2 carrots, sliced thin
3 tablespoons butter
2 yellow zucchini, sliced thin
2 green zucchini, sliced thin
½ cup diced red pepper
1 tablespoon chives
2 tablespoons Strawberry-Mint
    Vinegar
1 teaspoon vegetable salt
    (in health-food section)
¼ teaspoon ground black pepper

Sauté carrots in butter for 3 minutes. Add the remaining vegetables. Sauté until vegetables are just beginning to soften. Add the rest of the ingredients and cook about 5 more minutes, or until sauce begins to thicken a little. Serves 6.

Strawberry Vinaigrette

I love this vinaigrette on grilled chicken salad.

1 tablespoon minced onion
½ cup light olive oil
⅓ cup corn oil
¼ cup Strawberry-Mint Vinegar
1½ teaspoons coarse (kosher) salt
½ teaspoon cracked black pepper
½ teaspoon dry mustard
½ teaspoon sugar
1 tablespoon parsley
1 teaspoon dried mint
1 coddled egg

Blend all ingredients in a blender. Sprinkle on chicken salad. Keeps well in refrigerator 3 or 4 days. Makes 1 cup.

Lemon-Thyme Oil

I really like the flavor of light olive oil, but you can use whatever strength you prefer.

1 lemon   Light olive oil
5 stems fresh thyme

Wash the lemon well. Remove the skin in long strips. Place the lemon strips and stems of thyme into a bottle with a cork top or tight-fitting cap. Pour in the oil to within ½ inch of the top of the bottle. Leave the oil for at least a week before using, shaking it a couple times a week to distribute the flavor. The oil will pick up more flavor the longer it sits. When the flavor reaches the strength you desire, remove the thyme and lemon. Use for salad dressings, sautéing, or basting meat or poultry. Store in a cool, dark place.

64

© Guy Powers/Envision

Veal Piccata

This is a nice way to have veal that takes only minutes to prepare.

1½ pounds veal
½ cup flour
1 tablespoon unsalted butter
2 tablespoons Lemon-Thyme Oil
2 tablespoons diced scallion
¼ cup vermouth
½ lemon, sliced thinly and then each slice cut in half
Salt to taste
Freshly ground black pepper to taste
Fresh parsley, minced

Cut veal into 2-inch pieces and pound until very thin. Dredge veal in flour. Melt butter in fry pan and add the oil. Sauté the veal quickly until brown on both sides. Do this fast because you do not want to overcook the veal. Remove veal and keep warm. Add scallions to frying pan and sauté 2 minutes. Add the vermouth and lemon slices and cook 2 more minutes. Add salt and pepper to taste and pour sauce over veal. Sprinkle with parsley. Serves 4.

Crab Salad in Zucchini Boats

This salad is also good inside a pita bread with a big piece of lettuce added.

3 zucchini
Lemon-Thyme Oil
Salt and pepper to taste
1 pound crab meat
⅓ cup diced red pepper
2 tablespoons minced scallion
¼ cup diced celery
¼ cup diced cucumber
Lemon pepper to taste
½ teaspoon thyme
½ cup Lemon-Thyme Oil

2 tablespoons rice vinegar
½ avocado, diced small
½ tomato, peeled, seeded, and
  diced small

Wash zucchini and steam whole for 5 minutes. Remove and rinse in cold water. Cut zucchini lengthwise and scoop out seeds. Brush lightly with Lemon-Thyme Oil and sprinkle with salt and fresh ground pepper. Set aside.

Mix crab meat with red pepper, scallion, celery, and cucumber. Add lemon pepper, salt, thyme, Lemon-Thyme Oil, and rice vinegar. Toss well.

Divide crab salad among the 6 zucchini halves. Combine avocado and tomato dice. Put a spoonful of the dice on top of each zucchini. Serves 6.

Marinated Cucumbers

These cucumbers are great as one item on a composed salad dish or just as a side dish. This marinade is just as good on mushrooms or radishes.

4 long English (seedless) cucumbers
1 garlic clove, minced
2 tablespoons minced onion
1 teaspoon salt
1 tablespoon sugar
¼ cup Lemon-Thyme Oil
3 tablespoons rice vinegar
3 tablespoons sherry
1½ tablespoons soy sauce
½ teaspoon thyme

Slice cucumbers paper thin. Mix garlic, onion, salt, sugar, oil, vinegar, sherry, soy sauce, and thyme in a food processor or blender. Pour marinade over cucumbers, toss well, and chill at least 2 hours. Serves 12.

Marinated Cucumbers make a great side dish for a beautiful buffet.

© Dan Wilby

© Brian Leatart

66

Garlic Olive Oil

You need to acidify your garlic before using it so it does not become rancid. Do this by covering the garlic with vinegar for 24 hours. Don't throw away the vinegar because it is wonderful to use in your favorite salad dressing.

8 garlic cloves   Olive oil
White wine vinegar

Peel garlic and cut off ends. Score a little x in each clove. Pour enough white wine vinegar to cover the garlic and let it sit for 24 hours. Remove garlic from vinegar and put garlic in a clean bottle with a tight cork or tight-fitting lid. Fill the bottle with oil to within ½ inch of the top. Let oil sit for a week or more, shaking the bottle every 3 or 4 days. When the oil reaches the strength you want, remove garlic, except 1 or 2 cloves. Store in a cool, dark place.

Chinese Noodle Stirfry

You can find the Chinese egg noodles in the Oriental section of your supermarket. If you can't find them use any thin noodle. You can add cooked chicken or flank steak sliced thinly to this dish for variety.

6 ounces Chinese egg noodles
3 tablespoons Garlic Olive Oil
½ medium onion, sliced
1 zucchini, julienned
1 celery stalk, julienned
1 carrot, julienned
1 cup bean sprouts
½ cup snow peas
1 beef bouillon cube
⅓ cup water
¾ teaspoon sugar
⅓ cup soy sauce
3 teaspoons cornstarch
1 teaspoon black bean sauce
2 tablespoons rice vinegar

Boil noodles according to package directions. Drain. Then fry noodles in hot wok in oil. Remove noodles. In oil, sauté onion, zucchini, celery, carrot, sprouts, and snow peas until vegetables just turn soft. Add noodles and toss. In a separate bowl, mix bouillon, water, sugar, soy sauce, cornstarch, black bean sauce, and vinegar. Blend well and add to vegetables. Toss well and cover. Cook for 2 minutes. Cooked meat can be added if desired. Remove top and continue cooking until slightly thickened. Serves 4.

Grilled Quail Salad

Marinate quails overnight so the flavors penetrate the meat.

½ cup Garlic Olive Oil
2 tablespoons tequila
Juice from 2 limes
1½ teaspoons salt
1 teaspoon pepper
2 bay leaves, crushed
2 tablespoons minced onion
8 quail
8 leaves red leaf lettuce
1 head radicchio
1 bunch arugula
2 heads Belgian endive
1 avocado, diced small
1 ripe mango, diced small
2 tomatoes, diced

Dressing:
½ cup Garlic Olive Oil
1 tablespoon rice vinegar
2 tablespoons lime juice
½ medium tomato, diced
1 tablespoon sugar
1 tablespoon minced onion
1 teaspoon salt
1 teaspoon ground pepper
1 teaspoon cilantro

Mix the Garlic Olive Oil, tequila, lime juice, salt, pepper, bay leaves, and onions. Pour over the quail, cover, and marinate for at least 24 hours.

Remove quail from the marinade and grill quickly over very hot coals. There is not much to a quail so be sure you do not overcook; 6 to 7 minutes on each side is all they will need.

Tear red leaf lettuce, radicchio, arugula, and endive greens into bite-sized pieces. Cut avocado, mango, and tomatoes and sprinkle over salad. Lay quail on top of salad, leaving whole.

Make dressing by mixing oil, vinegar, lime juice, tomato, sugar, onion, salt, pepper, and cilantro in a blender or food processor. Drizzle the dressing over the salad. Serves 8.

67

© Dan Wilby

Stirfrying is an easy and fast way to cook delicious meals that are fresh-tasting and colorful.

Raspberry Mustard

This is a great all-purpose mustard.

¾ cup dry mustard	3 tablespoons sugar
2 tablespoons mustard seed	2 teaspoons salt
⅔ cup water	⅓ cup raspberry purée

Whirl the dry mustard, mustard seed, and water in a food processor. Add sugar and salt. Let sit covered overnight. The next day add the raspberry purée and process again. Put into little jars with tight-fitting lids or corks. Store in the refrigerator for up to 1 month. Makes 2¼ cups.

68

Spinach Salad with Sweet Mustard Dressing

I love spinach salad and this is a good one. If you make this salad and you are using your barbecue for the main course, throw some red potatoes on the grill and put them in the salad. The grilled flavor is a great addition. In the summer, a few fresh raspberries on top of each salad adds a spectacular touch.

Spinach, torn in bite-size pieces
Hard boiled eggs, minced
Tomatoes, diced
Mushrooms, sliced
Bacon, fried crisp and crumbled
Red onion rings
Pine nuts

Dressing:
2 tablespoons minced onion
2 tablespoons honey
1 teaspoon salt
½ teaspoon pepper
1 teaspoon Raspberry Mustard
1 tablespoon poppy seeds
½ cup vegetable oil
2 tablespoons Strawberry-Mint Vinegar (see page 62)
1 teaspoon celery seed

Layer salad ingredients in a bowl.

Make dressing by blending all ingredients in a blender. Makes 1½ cups dressing.

Sweet Mustard Dressing is the perfect complement to fresh spinach.

KITCHEN METRICS

For cooking and baking convenience, use the following metric measurements.
The table gives approximate, rather than exact, conversions.

Spoons:

1/4 teaspoon	=	1 milliliter
1/2 teaspoon	=	2 milliliters
1 teaspoon	=	5 milliliters
1 tablespoon	=	15 milliliters
2 tablespoons	=	25 milliliters
3 tablespoons	=	50 milliliters

Cups:

1/4 cup	=	50 milliliters
1/3 cup	=	75 milliliters
1/2 cup	=	125 milliliters
2/3 cup	=	150 milliliters
3/4 cup	=	175 milliliters
1 cup	=	250 milliliters
1 pint	=	500 milliliters
1 quart	=	1 liter

Oven Temperatures:

200° F = 100° C		350° F = 180° C
225° F = 110° C		375° F = 190° C
250° F = 120° C		400° F = 200° C
275° F = 140° C		425° F = 220° C
300° F = 150° C		450° F = 230° C
325° F = 160° C		475° F = 240° C

WEIGHT AND MEASURE EQUIVALENTS

1 inch = 2.54 centimeters
1 square inch = 6.45 square centimeters
1 foot = .3048 meters
1 square foot = 929.03 square centimeters
1 yard = .9144 meters
1 square yard = .84 square meters
1 ounce = 28.35 grams
1 pound = 453.59 grams

INDEX